School Effectiveness

Master Classes in Education Series

Series Editors: John Head, School of Education, Kings College, University of London and Ruth Merttens, School of Teaching Studies, University of North London

Working with Adolescents: Constructing Identity
John Head *Kings College, University of London*

Testing: Friend or Foe? The Theory and Practice of Assessment and Testing
Paul Black *Kings College, University of London*

Doing Research/Reading Research: A Mode of Interrogation for Education
Andrew Brown and Paul Dowling *both of the Institute of Education, University of London*

Educating the Other: Gender, Power and Schooling
Carrie Paechter *School of Education, The Open University*

Reflecting on School Management
Anne Gold and Jennifer Evans *both of the Institute of Education, University of London*

School Effectiveness: Fracturing the Discourse
Louise Morley *University of London* and Naz Rassool *University of Reading*

Master Classes in Education Series

School Effectiveness:
Fracturing the Discourse

Louise Morley and Naz Rassool

London and New York

First published 1999 by Falmer Press
11 New Fetter Lane, London EC4P 4EE

Simultaneously published in the USA and Canada
by Falmer Press
Routledge Inc, 29 West 35th Street, New York, NY 10001

Falmer Press is an imprint of the Taylor & Francis Group

© 1999 Louise Morley and Naz Rassool

Typeset in Garamond by Graphicraft Limited, Hong Kong
Printed and bound in Great Britain by TJ International Ltd, Padstow, Cornwall

British Library Cataloguing in Publication Data
A catalogue record for this book is available from the British Library

Library of Congress Cataloging in Publication Data
A catalogue record for this book has been requested

ISBN 0-750-70848-4 (hbk)
ISBN 0-750-70847-6 (pbk)

Contents

List of Figures

Series Editors' Preface

It has become a feature of our times that an initial qualification is no longer seen to be adequate for life-long work within a profession and programmes of professional development are needed. Nowhere is the need more clear than with respect to education, where changes in the national schooling and assessment system, combined with changes in the social and economic context, have transformed our professional lives.

The series, *Master Classes in Education*, is intended to address the needs of professional development, essentially at the level of taught masters degrees. Although aimed primarily at teachers and lecturers, it is envisaged that the books will appeal to a wider readership, including those involved in professional educational management, health promotion and youth work. For some, the texts will serve to up-date their knowledge. For others, they may facilitate career reorientation by introducing, in an accessible form, new areas of expertise or knowledge.

The books are overtly pedagogical, providing a clear track through the topic by means of which it is possible to gain a sound grasp of the whole field. Each book familiarizes the reader with the vocabulary and the terms of discussion, and provides a concise overview of recent research and current debates in the area. While it is obviously not possible to deal with every aspect in depth, a professional who has read the book should be able to feel confident that they have covered the major areas of content, and discussed the different issues at stake. The books are also intended to convey a sense of the future direction of the subject and its points of growth or change.

In each subject area the reader is introduced to different perspectives and to a variety of readings of the subject under consideration. Some of the readings may conflict, others may be compatible but distant. Different perspectives may well give rise to different lexicons and different bibliographies, and the reader is always alerted to these differences. The variety of frameworks within which each topic can be construed is then a further source of reflective analysis.

The authors in this series have been carefully selected. Each person is an experienced professional, who has worked in that area of education as a practitioner and also addressed the subject as a researcher and theoretician. Drawing upon both the pragmatic and the theoretical aspects of their experience, they are able to take a reflective view while preserving a sense of what occurs, and what is possible, at the level of practice.

School Effectiveness: Fracturing the Discourse

The current concern with school effectiveness is a tale starting with optimism and good intentions, but becoming increasingly more confused and controversial.

Go back 20 or 30 years and we find a widespread belief that schools and teachers had very limited opportunity to bring about educational improvement. Sociologists argued that many in society suffered such deprivation that high academic performance could not be expected from them. Psychologists at that time tended to subscribe to the notion that the capacity to learn was determined by certain fixed abilities, measured by intelligence tests or described in terms of Piagetian levels of cognitive development. All that schools and teachers could do in this event was to adjust to these realities.

Since that time there has been an accumulation of evidence that some schools are more successful than others, using a wide variety of measures of success, even when the schools are matched by intake and resources. Meanwhile psychologists, partly through the increasing recognition of the work of Russian writers such as Vygotsky, have recognized that there is considerable scope for teachers to effectively promote learning with their pupils.

Given these changes we can see why efforts have been made to identify and praise some schools and teachers and name and shame others. There have, however, been two problems. The first is that British schools are now subjected to more supervision and intervention than those in any other developed country, with a National Curriculum, testing at the four Key Stages, and inspection by OFSTED. Teachers find themselves responding to these external demands rather than dealing with what they see to be their real task. The second problem is that we are tending to value that which is measurable and contributes to the public image of the school. Pupils may now be excluded if they do not contribute to the school, whereas in the past they might have been nurtured. Parts of the curriculum which are not examined have become devalued, so far example, personal, social and health education have not fared well. People have ceased to ask whether pupils are happy and are enjoying their schooling – these are not measurable qualities. In the words of Wilde, we know 'the cost of everything and the value of nothing'.

Louise Morley and Naz Rassool have skilfully revealed the many strands of argument found in relation to this subject, providing clarity without denying the complexity, and giving an even handed analysis of the issues. The text has been enriched by them using both a historical and cross-cultural perspective to illuminate the issues. They provide an invaluable text for those seeking to understand the contemporary state of schooling in this country.

John Head and Ruth Merttens
January 1999

Chapter 1

Introduction: Shaping the Debate

As a theory of educational change, school effectiveness has generated a controversial body of knowledge, originating in industrialized countries such as Britain and the USA, and now exported throughout the developing world. It has become a vast industry, generating costly research and influencing educational policies in different national locations. In Britain, it has been part of the restructuring and modernizing interventions in the public services. It poses as a counterpoint to fuzzy thinking and imprecision in education and promises success criteria, with blueprints and taxonomies for the effective school. It offers advice on identifying bugs in the system and strategies for purification.

The school effectiveness movement is not new. It is the crystalization and reconfiguration of a range of belief systems, policy interventions and ideologies that have floated through education since at least the 1960s. As a bricolage – or patchwork – deriving from different ideologies, pressures and logics, school effectiveness has reclassified and reformulated ideas, concerns, panics and prejudices. For several decades attempts have been made to isolate and identify the crucial factors in education that promote academic achievement. Different ideological and political interest groups have all advocated different strategies for ensuring value for money in education. The economics of education, with concerns about economic and social returns of educational investment, have played a central part in the debates on school effectiveness and academic achievement. School effectiveness has also gained international currency (Fuller, 1987; Fuller and Clarke, 1994). Software packages have been developed for use in developing countries and an international traffic in consultancy and evaluation has emerged. In such diverse global contexts, it is questionable whether a universal formula for educational change can exist.

The ascendancy of school effectiveness as a dominant educational discourse has both been enabled and forged in the West by the enterprise culture of the late 1980s and 1990s. There has been a reconfiguration of power, and a key question is whether the discourses of school effectiveness and improvement constitute new regimes of truth and domination. The school effectiveness movement, and, more recently, its operational arm – school improvement – are sometimes seen as utilitarian solutions to a largely manufactured crisis over standards. Hamilton (1998: 13) suggests that school effectiveness is 'social Darwinist' and 'eugenic', standing at 'the intersection of educational research and social engineering'. School effectiveness is characterized by product champions (e.g. Mortimore et al., 1988; Sammons, Hillman and Mortimore, 1995; Reynolds, 1996) and equally vociferous critics (e.g. Angus, 1993; Ball, 1995; Elliot, 1996; Fielding, 1997; Slee, Weiner and Tomlinson, 1998). With a few exceptions, the majority of voices in the debate have been male, and a certain machismo has been attached to the hegemonic warfare over educational policy and standards.

We are not against the raising of educational standards. We wish to argue that educational change is more complex than the improvement of examination results. Setting the context for the rest of the book, this chapter will outline the genesis of the school effectiveness movement, and in the tradition of policy archaeology, it will intertextually trace the historical origins of the debate on standards, public accountability and measurement. That is, it will identify how different texts, documents and popular beliefs influenced each other to produce the current concern with standards and value for money in education. While the emphasis in Britain, under New Labour, is now on stakeholding and social inclusion, there is still a strong continuity between the educational project of the current and previous administrations.

Binary Thinking

The concern for school effectiveness has been of political importance in the West since at least the 1960s, when the Coleman Report (1966) in the USA, and the Plowden Report (1967) in Britain investigated patterns of academic success and failure in different primary schools. A central finding in both documents was the role that socio-economic and family backgrounds played in facilitating educational success. Coleman conducted a large scale survey of the achievement of 645,000 students in 4000 primary and secondary schools. His findings indicated that academic attainment was largely independent of the schooling a child received.

Since the early 1970s, the school effectiveness movement has made strenuous efforts to demonstrate that Coleman was wrong, and that schools do make a difference. One of the founders of the school effectiveness movement in the USA, the black educator, Ron Edmonds, rejected the Coleman Report's findings and argued that 'all children are eminently educable and . . . the behaviour of the school is critical in determining the quality of that education' (Edmonds, 1979: 20). Edmonds attempted to act against the pessimism of social determinism and ensure that schools did not lower their expectations of black children. More recently in Britain, Michael Barber, a leading figure in school effectiveness, and now an adviser to the Labour Government, wrote about the new culture of monitoring, review and improvement:

> The new view, now that we know schools make a difference, dictates a
> different logic. It requires teachers, individually and collectively, to review

Figure 1.1: Binary thinking

Bi-polar Classifications in School Effectiveness Framework	Product Champions' Measurement Instruments	Critics Dismiss School Effectiveness As
effective/failing schools	characteristics	positivistic
good/bad teachers	taxonomies	evangelical
traditional/progressive teaching methods	typologies	socially decontextualized
universal panacea/common sense	certainty, exactitude and authority	a new regime of truth – displacing concerns about equity
old/new regimes	factors	simplistic common sense
organizational/socio-economic factors	checklists	technicist

what they do and to try and improve it. The research on school effectiveness has thus contributed to a fundamental and wholly welcome change of climate. Teachers and schools now believe they can make a difference; they can work towards changes which are achievable and whose effects can be monitored. (Barber, 1996: 128)

Much of the debate on school effectiveness has been posed in terms of a conceptual hierarchy of bivalence (see Figure 1.1). There is an abundance of binary oppositions in this means/ends construction, with an assumed unity of purpose, values and goals. For example, schools and teachers are either good or bad, effective or failing (Ball, 1997). Educational success has been reduced to factors that can be measured. Explanatory variables identified in research findings have constantly shifted between the psycho-social focus on the family on the one hand and organizational factors on the other. The current skew is towards the organizational, with a belief in the capacity of bureaucratic co-ordination to deliver predictable outputs (Clarke and Newman, 1997). With measurement, accountability and evaluation has come a new morality of attainment (Strathern, 1997). A particular performance of schools, teachers and students has become a register of truth about effectiveness. In this technical-rationalist framework, a teacher's actions are judged as valuable only if they bring about what is perceived as education's proper ends (Parker, 1997). The new classification is based on a new moral authority with quantification and inevitable casualties. Barber (1996) notes how 170 schools (between 1–2 per cent of the total) have been found to be 'failing' since the national four-year inspection cycle began in Britain in 1996. He also estimates how a further 1250–2500 schools were just below the 'failing' category. He concluded with the 'terrifying statistic' (1996: 123) that 'one state school in eight is providing its pupils with an inadequate education'. The sensationalization of the problem has enabled the development of an elaborate machinery to bring about a cure.

The Values Drift in Education

As we indicated in Figure 1.1, the effectiveness discourse itself is perceived as either the universal panacea for educational ills, or dismissed as too technicist and positivistic to be of interest. However, since New Right education reform in both the USA and UK in the 1980s, there have been foundational changes in educational policy, underpinned by 'politically-fuelled moral panics about "failing" teachers in "failing" schools' (Hargreaves and Evans, 1997: 2). In Britain, the Department for Education and Employment now has a school effectiveness division. However, the school effectiveness movement comprises many voices and strands. It has become a disciplinary force and a powerful transitional rhetoric differently appropriated and incorporated to reflect differing ideologies. As we stated, the concerns and logic of school effectiveness are not new. It is a working example of how words and phrases can change in discourse, depending on the site from which they are articulated (Pecheux, 1982). Whereas the New Right introduced effectiveness as a strategy to control the ideological content of education, New Labour claim to use it in the context of standards and as a tool for challenging social differentiation and promoting social inclusion.

The discourse of school effectiveness gained increased prominence in the 1980s, as part of New Right reform in Britain and the USA. However, by this time, there had been a values drift, with emphasis shifting away from social and cultural considerations, to the study of the school as an organization. Social theories were perceived as over-deterministic, and social disadvantages were thought possible to overcome by appropriate forms of educational management. In their study, Mortimore, Stoll, Sammons and Ecob (1988) argue that primary schools with similar intakes performed very differently. For example, middle-class children in the least effective schools did noticeably worse than working-class children in the most effective. The declared impetus for changes in policy and practices revolved around the concepts of raising standards in education.

Under the pressures of global competition, many countries became increasingly concerned about the performance of their educational systems. For example, in a technological age, it was felt to be of vital importance to ensure that Britain did not lose out to other industrialized economies as a consequence of a relatively unskilled workforce. According to research undertaken by the Institute of Employment in the UK, by the year 2000, 70 per cent of all jobs in Europe will require people with A levels and above (Day, 1997). There are strong beliefs that Britain needs to overhaul its educational system in order to be more globally competitive. This has been a central theme in New Labour's White Paper (DfEE, 1997). Workplace restructuring, or microeconomic reform, has become conceptually linked to enhanced productivity.

Furthermore, the discourse of failure that has emerged since the 1980s corresponds with other socio-cultural factors of the risk society (Beck, 1992). Failing schools and failing teachers are perceived as risks to the public, in much the same way as faulty engines on aircraft. There is now considerable emphasis on high reliability organizations, with zero defects in the products and processes (Reynolds, 1996; Slee, 1998). Teacher autonomy has been reduced and new regulatory processes have been introduced to scrutinize teachers' work. As a consequence, educators have had to negotiate a litany of changes: new managerialism; new forms of assessment; new partnerships e.g. with school governors, employers and parents. Teachers are held responsible for alleged falling educational standards, plus a range of social ills such as youth crime, violence, young people's alienation and disaffection. Paradoxically, teachers are both burdened with enormous social responsibility, while simultaneously being constructed as professionally wanting.

The solution has been an attempt to make education teacher-proof. Elmore and McLaughlin (1988) note how many policy processes substitute external authority for the expertise of educational practitioners. Paradoxically, policies need to be implemented by the very people who are often excluded, objectified or treated with contempt in the policy process. This has involved intense regulation via school inspections, reports and in extreme cases, school closures. There has been a reconstruction of the teacher and teaching. Parker (1997: 9) argues that:

> The teacher is seen as essentially a means-ends broker and teaching is conceived as a technical exercise, an applied science, concerned with, and judged according to, the criteria of means-ends efficiency.

Two bodies of theory have emerged: school effectiveness and school improvement. A key difference between school effectiveness and school improvement is that the former believes that outcomes of achievement or behaviour can vary between schools dealing with similar kinds of pupil population. It is particularly concerned with *measurement*. School improvement is more concerned with *processes* of change, such as School Development Plans. The language and ethos of both school effectiveness and improvement often appear to have quasi religious connotations, implying lack, deficit or original sin. Strathern (1997: 307) writes:

> 'Improvement' is wonderfully open-ended, for it at once describes efforts and results. And it invites one to make both ever more effective – a process from which the tests themselves are not immune: measuring the improvement leads to improving the measures.

There is a major question here about the endpoint for school improvement and effectiveness, with an underlying sense of the permanence of struggle, the elusiveness of satisfactory goals, and the ambiguity of measurement procedures.

The rhetoric of school effectiveness starts with an assumption of guilt. This is in sharp contrast with the language associated with learning organizations, which often emphasises creativity and expansion. Senge (1990: 3) describes learning organizations as:

organizations where people continually expand their capacity to create the results they truly desire, where new and expansive patterns of thinking are nurtured, where collective aspiration is set free and where people are continually learning how to learn together.

In this analysis, there are vastly different constructions of employee motivation, raising questions about whether change stems from creativity, support and high expectations or fear, guilt and blame. For example, proponents of school effectiveness and improvement note how the public shaming of 'failing' schools can galvanize them into taking drastic measures (Barber, 1996). The school effectiveness and school improvement movements are seen to provide a sense of direction for 'lost' schools. There is a reinvention thesis in which failing schools can be reborn. They may be sinners, but they can confess, purge and renew themselves. The Department for Education and Employment has indicated that the rate of improvement is greatest among those schools which are in the bottom 25 per cent in terms of performance (*TES*, 6 October, 1995). The moral undertones of schools being expected to self-examine and confess to difficulties/problems is reminiscent of Foucauldian concepts of discipline and punishment.

An essential ingredient in school effectiveness is the shift from the social to the organizational context, from the macro to the microculture. The school is represented largely as a bounded institution, set apart, but also in a precarious relationship with a broader social context. It is ironic that, at a time when social disadvantage appears to be increasing in Britain, school effectiveness theory places less emphasis on poverty, deprivation and social exclusion, and more emphasis on organizational factors such as professional leadership, home/school partnerships, the monitoring of academic progress, shared vision and goals. At the same time, the influential Rowntree Report (1995) identified that one third of children in Britain live in families with an income under half the national income and a fifth live on income support. In addition, the UK has one of the lowest levels of investment in public housing in Europe, and according to the International Labour Office, there is a higher proportion of people unemployed in the world than at any time since the 1930s (Day, 1997). A central assumption in much of the thinking on school effectiveness is that absolute standards are attainable. Furthermore, these are neutral, value-free and socially decontextualized. While equity theories in education made important links between social identity and cognitive ability, school effectiveness appears to have overlooked power/knowledge conjunctions.

The Origins of the Discourse: 1960s Expansion and the Opening of Minds and Purses

The 1960s were a period of unprecedented growth and the education service expanded more rapidly than the public economy as a whole. However, it soon became apparent that the 1944 Education Act, with its commitment to equal opportunity for all, had not succeeded in eliminating educational inequalities. While general educational levels were rising, marked social class differentials in academic attainment remained (Banting, 1985). For example, the Robbins Committee on Higher Education reported that children of fathers in professional and managerial occupations were 20 times more likely to enter university than those of fathers in semi-skilled or unskilled jobs (Robbins, 1963). At that time, mothers' occupations or educational qualifications were not considered. New challenges to the views of 1930s educational psychologists were also being offered. Whereas the Hadow Report (1926) and the Spens Report (1938) accepted the belief that cognitive ability was innate, the post-war period witnessed the beginnings of educational sociology.

The 1960s were a time of radical change and moral panics. Disquiet about selection at 11 and the effectiveness of the 11-plus examination began to emerge. Comprehensive schooling was introduced in 1965 by a Labour Government ostensibly committed to educational equity. Several important committees of inquiry were formed in this period. In 1963, the Plowden Inquiry was set up to look at primary education. Two of its members were sociologists, David Donnison and Michael Young. One aspect of the committee's work was to examine social influences on educational attainment. In addition to promoting 'child-centred' education, the Plowden Report, published in 1967, called for a national policy of 'positive discrimination'; deprived urban areas should be designated 'educational priority areas' and should receive the most generous and innovative educational provision. Clarke and Newman (1997: 12) argue that:

> . . . the crisis of the social penetrated deeply into the organisational and occupational worlds of the 'old' welfare state.

The move towards compensatory education was contentious from the point of educational economics, as there was little hard evidence linking investment of resources with enhanced academic results. It could be argued that the school effectiveness movement, emerged in response to this, with a belief that investment in schools as organizations could counter social disadvantages. A remediation ethos evolved, within the welfare interventionist approaches advocated within this compensatory model of education. There was also a juxtaposition of urban with poverty – a feature which ignored deprivation located elsewhere. The 1960s saw the development of a long-running, heated debate on the relative importance of genetic or environmental factors, and the extent to which education can compensate for social deprivation. The essentialism (nature) versus social construction of achievement (nurture) debate has been a critical element in policy development.

Another influential document was the Newsom Report (Ministry of Education, 1963). Its focus was the so-called less or non-academic student. The then Conservative Secretary of State for Education, Sir Edward Boyle, wrote a social constructionist foreword to the Newsom Report and stated that he 'accepted the view that "intelligence" could be "acquired" and was not therefore a fixed quantity impervious to any educational influence' (cited in Chitty, 1989: 37). Boyle argues:

> . . . the essential point is that all children should have an equal opportunity of acquiring intelligence, and of developing their talents and abilities to the full. (Ministry of Education, 1963: iv)

The post-war transition from essentialism to social construction theories raised crucial questions about which aspects of the social could be amenable to intervention.

The 1970s: Sociology and Standards

Kogan (1985: 17) cites the 1970s as the beginning of a period of 'bringing schools under greater political and central control'. The preoccupation with standards was introduced as a counter to decades of 'trendy education theory' (Goodson, 1997). 'Progressive' methods were thought to have shifted the educational agenda away from concerns about efficacy of classroom practices, and into the more nebulous realms of social justice, equality, and personal development. There was continuing suspicion that child-centred approaches advocated by Plowden in the 1960s were not resulting in enhanced academic achievement, particularly in reading and arithmetic. In the USA, Jencks' famous study on inequality (1972) reported its findings in terms of *measurement* of the school factor. He concluded that 'equalizing the quality of high schools would reduce cognitive inequality by one per cent or less'. Commenting on the input/output dimension of compensatory education, he asserted that 'additional school expenditures are unlikely to increase achievement, and redistributing resources will not reduce test score inequality'.

As we will argue in Chapter 2, the political economy of education was also influenced in the 1970s by the oil crisis in 1973. This marked the beginning of stringent economies in the public sector. There was a more pronounced intersection of economics and politics, and a dislocation and destabilization of the Keynesian post-war settlement. Unemployment was rising, and resources had to be differently deployed as the period of economic expansion started to close.

The raising of educational standards was to become a central policy objective for the Labour Government and 1974 saw the introduction of the Assessment of Performance Unit (APU). As we discuss in Chapter 2, in 1976, James Callaghan, the then Labour Prime Minister, made his famous Ruskin College speech. This speech was perceived as the opening of the 'Great Debate' and impetus for the Green Paper, *Education in Schools* (DES, 1977). The paper argued for a period of stability after comprehensive reorganization, in order for standards to improve.

The year 1976 also saw the publication of the controversial report on teaching styles in primary schools (Bennett, 1976).

> The main conclusion of this report was that pupils taught by so-called 'formal' methods (class taught, in silence, with regular testing and a good deal of healthy competition) were, on average, four months ahead of those taught by 'informal' methods according to tests in the basic skills in English and mathematics. (Chitty, 1989: 65)

There was considerable criticism of this study, particularly for its over-simplified classification of teaching methods (Galton, Simon and Croll, 1980). However, as it contained all the elements of a 'good story', the media ignored the criticisms and gave substantial coverage to the 'failure' of progressive methods.

More attempts were made to identify key factors in educational attainment. Rutter et al.'s influential study of secondary education in Inner London (1979: 180) suggested that there is a 'causal relationship between school process and children's progress'. They raised questions about the pattern of correlations with school processes:

> The question here is whether schools were as they were because of the children they admitted, or rather whether children behaved the way they did because of school influences. (Rutter et al., 1979: 181)

Whereas Rutter et al. identified institutional bias, or school ethos, as an important constituent in school effectiveness, Her Majesty's Inspectorate (1978) reported that teachers' subject expertise and the quality of their teaching interrelated in the production of high student achievement.

Meanwhile, findings from sociology of education, particularly those of Bernstein (1971, 1977) and Bourdieu (1977) demonstrated how schools, as social institutions, mediate between macro- and micro-society. Bernstein's famous saying, 'education cannot compensate for society' entered the frame (Bernstein, 1970). By exposing how schools institutionalized cultural privilege and middle class values, language and codes, sociologists of education explored how schools played an active role in cultural reproduction. This view contradicted mobility studies which represented schools as politically and socially neutral institutions. In the latter analysis, education was perceived as inherently a good thing to which socially disadvantaged groups should gain enhanced and equitable access. However, several key studies in the 1970s established how schools allocate students, on the basis of their social class, to educational opportunity and to their designated places in employment and social status. In the USA, Bowles and Gintis (1976) used correspondence theory to identify how educational settings mirror conditions in the workplace, which are themselves hierarchical and socially deterministic (Angus, 1993). Rather than providing equal opportunities for all students regardless of background, schools merely reproduced the unequal relations from wider society. This Marxist study, while exposing the subtleties of cultural reproduction, was also criticized for its pessimism and social determinism. Socially deprived young people were represented as passive victims of dominant social structures.

In Britain, the influential ethnography conducted by Paul Willis (1977) confirmed that while white, working class boys attend school fundamentally in order to learn to labour, they also evolved elaborate strategies of resistance, with sophisticated subcultural codes and values. Hence, a sociological debate on the dialectical relationship between structures and agency focused discussion on social production, as well as social reproduction. Angus (1993: 335) points out how sociology of education:

> . . . has been rich and varied, and, in the main, has amounted to a reflexive, interpretive, analytical and extraordinarily diverse movement, as researchers have attempted to understand and explain the complex notion of 'what counts' as educational practice and its relation to the social formation.

Immigration from the Caribbean, the Indian Sub-Continent and East Africa also meant that school populations were changing. This presented new challenges to the process of schooling, the curriculum, language, teaching methods and school values, prejudices and beliefs. It injected more 'chaos' to be managed by the system, and exposed the parochialism of many attitudes and approaches to teaching and learning.

Regulation and Surveillance: The 1980s and Education Reform

It has been argued that after the 1944 Education Act, the 1988 Education Reform Act (ERA) has been the most influential piece of educational policy this century (Ball, 1994). Unemployment and economic crises in industrialized nations in the late 1970s and early 1980s raised questions about the relevance and adequacy of education systems in so-called developed nations. Restructuring became part of an international agenda, in response to globalization, i.e. the rapid growth in technologies, the compression of time and space, and shifting modes of economic production (Woods et al., 1997). Reform and restructuring contained a complex mixture of enhanced central regulation and ostensible decentralization. The Department of Education and Science (DES) in 1984 withheld local authority money and used it to promote curriculum development schemes of its own choice. Hysteria over standards and the risks incurred by 'poor' teaching led to threats by the Secretary of State in 1985 to enforce the competence testing of teachers.

The 1987 Election Manifesto for the British Conservative Party highlighted four specific reforms: a national curriculum, local control of school budgets, parental choice of school, and the provision of mechanisms for schools to opt out of the control of Local Education Authorities. A massive process of reculturing ensued. Educational reform in the 1980s introduced the concept of the market into education. As we will indicate in Chapters 4 and 5, systems theory was beginning to gain considerable influence in the way education was managed. Managerialism and the enterprise culture started to gain currency, and, by the mid-1980s, HMI were advocating increasing the management strategies of evaluation, strategic planning and teacher appraisal (Department of Education and Science, 1985). As Woods et al. (1997: 10) suggest:

> The influential discussion paper, *Curriculum Organisation and Classroom Practice* (DES, 1992), conveyed a model of the 'good' teacher as not restricted to one having competency and qualities to facilitate work in classrooms, but one that also has managerial competencies.

Ten years after the Ruskin speech, a national core curriculum was introduced. The ERA also reinforced the notion of examination as the formal testing and signifier of ability. Examinations, once again, were perceived as neutral instruments for making levels of attainment visible, both for individual students, and schools as organizations.

Another crucial aspect of 1980s policy agenda was the principle of decentralization. Under the Local Management of Schools (LMS), responsibility for budget and a range of management tasks have been devolved to schools. As independent budget-holders, locally managed schools receive funding according to the number and ages of students on roll. It was widely believed that delegating responsibility for financial management to headteachers would release entrepreneurial initiative (Grace, 1995). Competition was also seen as a catalyst for creativity and the eventual raising of educational standards. The public services were no longer to be state monopolies, with ensured producer capture. They would have to compete to attract clients and state funding would follow performance. Crucial to this argument is the notion of informed choice. This means that indicators are required both to demonstrate value for money, and also to inform consumers about the quality and effectiveness of the educational product that they are purchasing. In a market economy, emphasis on consumer empowerment and entitlements (Morley, 1995) has led to increasing preoccupation with accountability, measurement, outcomes, performance indicators and results. Educational reform in the 1980s was a triumph for the New Right, with its ideological commitment to self-reliance. As one such advocate states:

> . . . the Education Reform Act of 1988 has at least shaken the system up. Competition and choice have been injected into it as a vaccination against bureaucratic inertia. . . . The worst excesses of the politicized curriculum of the sixties and seventies have been challenged and limited. A beginning has even been made . . . on assessing the effectiveness of teaching and learning. (Marsland, 1995: 23)

The 1990s – Rhetoric of Choice and Entitlements

In the 1990s, school effectiveness researchers have moved away from consideration of sociological factors, and towards a quest for student achievement indicators. In school effectiveness, schools are often perceived as largely detached from their social contexts. The core of research is to identify and isolate variables, techniques and procedures that can be transferred to any school and to any management system. The process of measurement has been married with quantification, that is, the numerical summary of attainment, presented in the form of league tables, to ensure that examination results are permanently available for inspection.

League tables were introduced by the Conservative Government for the first time for secondary examinations in 1993, and extended to primary schools in 1996. The aim was to produce a sense of certainty and exactitude, as well as to reinforce the notion of a critical external gaze. For example, if academic performance could be measured, then targets, goals, outcomes could be identified and worked for. After decades of uncertainty about the magical ingredients involved in educational attainment, it appeared that there had been a major decoding, posed in rational, technical terms. The checklists and taxonomies of characteristics can provide some degree of rationality and assurance for purchasers and providers in a complex, changing and often irrational social world. Equally, positive inspections and quantified positions in league tables can provide teachers with a form of validation and recognition for their work – a type of educational hallmarking.

The school effect could now be measured. In a study of 94 secondary schools, Sammons, Thomas and Mortimore (1995) found that the difference between the most and the least effective schools was over 12 GCSE points for an average student. This is the equivalent of achieving six grade B GCSEs rather than six grade Ds. The notion of examination has been extended from a focus on individual students to examination of educational institutions themselves. So, it is no longer just a question of the student's academic performance, but also the organizational arrangements for getting students to that point.

Consumerism and the commodification of education have been features of the 1990s. There is now an emphasis on parental choice and competition, rather than on equity and redistributive social justice (Adler, Petch and Tweedie, 1989; Ball, 1993; Chubb and Moe, 1992; Whitty, Power and Halpin, 1997; Woods, 1992). Choices are constrained and articulated via a complex combination of material, cultural and social factors. However, by presenting education reform as consumer-oriented change, the value base of partisan advantage has been heavily disguised. The political economy of choice can be directly related to post-1980s human capital theories. For example, education, in the form of qualifications and skill development, is constructed as a major form of capital, leading to enhanced lifechances. This justifies the notion of investment, or user-pay, such as the introduction of tuition fees for undergraduates in universities. Another dominant rhetoric in the public services in the 1990s is that of value for money and the need to ensure parsimony and accountability for public funds. School effectiveness and school improvement covertly imply a need to ensure the best possible returns on investment. Improvement and effectiveness are linked to commensurable increase. Strathern (1997: 308) points out how:

> The action of making something better, and thus *increasing* its value, elevating it in the sense of enhancement, had been built irrevocably into the term improvement.

Educational policy has also reflected this drive to refine, improve and insure against every eventuality. The volume of policies can also indicate crisis, mismanagement and hysteria. There was a proliferation of Education Acts in the 1990s as the Conservative party struggled to hold on to legitimacy. There was one Act in 1991, two in 1992, an extremely long one in 1993 and another in 1994. Under the 1992 Education Act, every school is required to be inspected every four years. This was extended to five years and then to six years under New Labour. The process is highly visible and the school is required to send a copy of the inspection report to every parent.

This book will question how academic achievement, success and failure are socially constructed. Underpinning the entire movement on standards, standardization and school effectiveness is the assumption that once a set of educational 'truths' has been established, they hold good for all teachers, schools, children, parents and communities. School effectiveness can represent an epistemology of closure and certainty. It is both a homogenized and homogenizing discourse. We aim to open up some discursive space. At the end of each chapter, we will raise some questions for discussion and reflection. Examining the issues identified here, this book will attempt to undertake a radical deconstruction of school effectiveness by fracturing the discourse. In so doing, it will interrogate what is hidden, contradictory, distorted and avoided in the common-sense rhetoric of school effectiveness.

Chapter 2 examines how quality and effectiveness are socially and politically constructed. It reflects on the impact of the 'Great Debate' in the 1970s, the 1988 ERA in the UK, and on conceptions of a 'successful' school. It investigates the way in which these articulated with earlier discourses on standards and effectiveness. It also critically examines how human capital theory and Total Quality Management have been incorporated into the economics of education. Chapter 3 explores the Japanization of education. That is, how mechanisms for quality assurance from industry have been introduced into the public services to guarantee zero defects and continuity of standards and outcomes. It locates school effectiveness and school improvement discourses within the broader framework of cultural and social change during the 1980s and 1990s. It discusses the flexibility discourse, the learning society, neo-Taylorism, New Labour's educational ideologies,

Figure 1.2: Policy origins of school effectiveness

Robbins Report 1963
Children of 'fathers' in professional and managerial occupations were 20 times more likely to enter HE than those of fathers in semi or unskilled jobs.

Newsom 1963
Recognition that 'intelligence could be acquired'.

Coleman 1966
Academic attainment was largely independent of schooling; it related to socio-economic backgrounds of families.

Plowden 1967
Compensatory, child-centred education, EPA areas, positive discrimination. Investment in schools could counter social deprivation.

Jencks' study on inequality, 1972
Additional school expenditures unlikely to increase achievement.

Callaghan's Ruskin speech, 1976
The beginning of the Great Debate, more overt political interventions re. value for money, links between education and employment, a core curriculum, raising standards.

Bennett's study on teaching methods, 1976
Main finding was that children taught by 'formal' methods, were on average, 4 months ahead of those taught by 'informal' methods in English and maths.

Bowles and Gintis, 1976
Cultural reproduction theory. Heavily criticized for social determinism.

Rutter et al.'s study of secondary education in Inner London, 1979.
This identified a 'causal relationship between school process and children's progress'.

LEA Equal Opportunities Policies, 1980s
Attempts to address structural inequalities such as gender and race via policy, curriculum, resources, teaching materials, employment, organizational culture etc.

Hargreaves Report, 1984
Identified the school as a system. Academic achievement could be managed.

1988 ERA
The introduction of marketization, competition, new managerialism, standardization and ending state monopolies. Concepts of quality assurance, measurement, performance. Key concepts are choice, empowerment, entitlements.

Policy 'hysteria' of 1990s
League tables introduced in secondary education in 1993, and in primary in 1996. School effectiveness researchers attempt to identify student achievement indicators.

---

post-Fordist work practices; research and development, Total Quality Management (TQM) and the Japanese production concept of *kaizen*.

Chapter 4 considers school effectiveness as an example of new managerialism in education. It identifies the model of change advanced during the 1980s, and examines key concepts and criteria for success identified within the discourse of management as well as the processes and practices through which these have operated. It deconstructs the audit explosion (Power, 1994), and critically looks at new systems of accountability and regulation. Chapter 5 provides an overview of school improvement discourses and identifies the main arguments of the debate. It considers the philosophical base of the notion of the school as a learning organization and frameworks for change such as institutional development plans. Chapter 6 outlines how school effectiveness has been exported and incorporated into educational policies in developing countries. It addresses the school effectiveness discourses structured within the educational policy framework of the World Bank and UNESCO, and considers these in relation to historical developments and prevailing social conditions within these societies. It asks whether school effectiveness is transferable and relevant in an international context.

Chapter 7 examines equity discourses grounded in the school effectiveness/ improvement frameworks. It discusses whether the social structures of gender, ethnicity, sexualities, disabilities and social class have been incorporated, distorted or excluded from effectiveness thinking. It also subjects the notion of empowerment to critique in relation to the range of meanings attached to it within organizational cultures and policies, and the interaction between these and wider social and cultural processes. Chapter 8 attempts to re-define educational change by identifying key issues to be considered in a framework for educational development that transcends technocratic models of change to incorporate perspectives of culture, politics and society. The book ends by concluding that school effectiveness, while appearing to be a neutral scientistic device, is indeed, saturated in power relations.

Chapter 2

Manufacturing the Crisis: The Social Construction of Quality and Standards in Contemporary Education

This chapter looks at the relationship between the meanings currently attached to notions of school effectiveness, and those constructed in previous educational discourse frameworks. This approach derives from Giddens' (1979: 70) view of intertextuality which states that although 'every process of action is a production of something new, a first act . . . all action exists in continuity with the past, which supplies the means of initiation'. In doing so, it aims to emphasize the relational nature of education. That is to say, that it is constituted in different sets of historically derived social relations that are circumscribed and sustained by power networks, practices and processes embedded in society and culture.

In particular, we want to focus on the categories of description and classification that have successively framed the debate about individual, social and institutional efficacy. Language mediates reality; it provides the terms of reference with which and through which we interpret and name the world in which we live. Language is therefore an important marker of social change. The language used to describe educational change and development provide important indicators regarding the nature and types of improvement advocated and supported. These invariably operate over and against other sets of meanings and possibilities. Key words, concepts and definitions related to issues of 'quality' and 'effectiveness' will be highlighted and examined in terms of their particular significations within different social and ideological milieux.

The chapter does not seek to engage with policy process, although we acknowledge the complexity of interactions within and through which different sets of meanings are derived at local level. Instead, the purpose of the chapter is to provide an overview of the discursive political discourses that have framed educational change and development during the past three decades. The intention overall is to examine their cumulative influence on shaping the terms and frame of reference of the new regulatory 'science' that has developed around the concepts of school effectiveness and school improvement. It will look at the ways in which meanings operating at macro-level have served to construct historically specific concepts of 'quality', 'standards' and 'effectiveness' as the basis of successful schools and schooling.

Education as Human Capital

The 1960s were not only an era of educational expansion but also a period of sustained debate about the social value of education. As seen in our introductory chapter, much of this discussion centred on the impact of socio-economic variables on educational success, and the need to facilitate equality of opportunity for those who had been socially and educationally disadvantaged. At the same time, the end of the economic boom during the late 1950s and early 1960s saw the ascendancy of the economics of education. Concerns about the social and economic returns of educational investment were to have a major impact on educational policy in England and Wales during the next three decades.

John Vaizey, an academic economist, initiated the debate about the cost-benefits of education in England and Wales. Arguing for increased levels of skill and the need for manpower (*sic*) planning as important components in national economic growth, Vaizey (1958: 68) held the view that:

> A rising national income requires a more skilled labour force to operate the economy, and therefore a rise in the educational attainments of that population, while at the same time releasing the resources for undertaking that education. This may be couched, in terms, especially, of trained manpower, to illustrate it forcefully.

Vaizey placed the development of 'human capital', that is, investment in 'manpower' as the basis of economic growth at the centre of his argument. Human capital theory emphasizes the direct relationship between education, worker productivity and the economy and is underscored by the principle that economic development can be maximized through a process of constructive educational planning. Underlining the need for increased investment in education Vaizey maintained that 'the returns on education both individually and socially, are at least as high as those in physical capital' (Vaizey, 1962: 38).

Human capital theory also received support elsewhere in the international arena at the time, notably in the area of post-colonial development theory (see Chapter 6). At the time, societal modernization provided the basis of the new economic development paradigm. The arguments were, first, that a modern economy increasingly dependent on modern technologies and scientific knowledge, would demand an adequate supply of educated 'manpower' having the requisite range of knowledges and skills to function in a largely industrialized labour market. Second, higher levels of education would increase productivity and this, in turn, was a key variable in stimulating national economic growth. The influential American agricultural economist, Theodore Schultz, argued that:

> The economic value of education rests on the proposition that people enhance their capabilities as producers and as consumers by investing in

themselves and that schooling is the largest investment in human capital. (Schultz, 1963: 10)

The modern industrial economy relied on the need for 'people to know far more than ever before and to be far more flexible, adaptable, and resilient to change' (Vaizey, 1962: 10). Speaking in the aftermath of the USSR's success in the Sputnik 'manned' space-flight, placing it at the forefront of scientific development internationally, Vaizey stated that:

> We live in a time when knowledge is exploding. More knowledge, new techniques, and new abilities have to be given to more and more people because of this fact. Knowledge and techniques are changing the world, and education must change with it. (Vaizey, 1961: 38)

What was also at stake was Britain's position within the international economy including its status as a trading partner and its role as a significant player in international markets. Education was seen as playing an important role in enabling 'this country to go forward by paying its way and competing internationally; but it is essential if we are to survive in a changing, technical and scientific age' (Vaizey, 1962: 12). This relationship between technology, science, social and economic development as the *raison d'être* of educational change was to be a recurring theme during the next few decades.

The human capital theme of investment in people was consolidated in the Labour Party's 1964 election manifesto. Emphasizing the need for the development of new work practices and worker awareness, Harold Wilson stated that:

> The Britain that is going to be forged in the white heat of this revolution will be no place for restrictive practices or outdated methods on either side of industry. (quoted in CCCS, 1981: 97)

The need for curricular and educational reform in order to cater for the knowledge and skills requirement of societal modernization was taken up in Harold Wilson's pre-election speeches. Human capital theory also featured centrally in Labour's National Plan of 1965 which stated that:

> Education is both an important social service and an investment for the future. It helps to satisfy the needs of the economy for skilled manpower of all kinds, the needs of any civilized society for educated citizens who have been enabled to develop to the utmost their individual abilities, and the demands by individuals for education as a means both to improved economic prospects and to a richer and more constructive life. (quoted in Chitty, 1989: 183)

Catering for the needs of the national economy, and facilitating personal efficacy were thus seen as ultimately serving the national interest.

Quality and Effectiveness

Within the macro-perspective adopted at the time, education and society as a whole provided the unit of analysis. That is to say, national economic and societal development provided global criteria by which the effectiveness and quality of education were to be judged. At the level of the school, effectiveness within the 'human capital' or modernization framework advocated by Vaizey, was seen primarily in terms of human resource management or 'manpower planning'. This included the efficient use of teachers facilitated by cost-effective, less labour intensive teaching methods such as team teaching and the use of programmed instruction in the use of teaching machines, television, language laboratories (Vaizey, 1967). Other factors revolved around the importance of raising educational productivity amongst high ability pupils, and reducing wastage related to pupil drop-out rate by using 'different methods of teaching, student aid, or counseling' for those who were less able (Vaizey and Debeauvais, 1961: 48). Advocacy of special treatment for the 'less able' coincided with the remediation ethos that prevailed generally in education at the time.

In line with Vaizey's views on the importance of 'manpower' planning, quality was defined principally in terms of having a highly qualified teaching staff (skilled 'manpower'), increased access to education (consumption), the need for educational planning ('manpower' forecasting) that responds effectively to labour market needs, and a broad curriculum that is relevant and can provide the skills needed in the modern industrial economy.

Two significant strands, namely, economy and cost-effectiveness, were now emerging to define the nature of a centrally planned, and managed, process of educational change. These meanings were to be legitimated in various defining sites and assume greater importance in different ideological frameworks over the next two decades.

Education and Moral Concerns: The Black Papers

By 1969 another theme entered the debate about schooling and education in a series of polemical pamphlets referred to as the *Black Papers*, published by a disparate group of contributors located largely within the Conservative Party. Their polemic comprised a moral crusade against a variety of issues including the social activist ethos of the period, youth subculture and social permissiveness which they blamed for the moral decay of the nation. They also criticized the principle of egalitarianism that underpinned the emergent comprehensive school system, as contributing to the lowering of educational standards.

Whereas the early *Black Papers* addressed a variety of issues related to the relationship between student culture and 'traditional social and political values and with social order' (Ball, 1990: 24), the later papers started the 'discourse of derision' (Ball, 1990: 31) on teachers and teaching. The main thrust was on structuring a moral panic around the perceived pedagogical deficiencies, moral irresponsibility and ideological dogmatism of teachers and administrators. Progressive child-centred teaching methods supported by many educationists and educational psychologists at the time, were singled out particularly as constituting a threat to school discipline and as undermining educational standards. According to Jones (1987: 8):

> The alleged inability of comprehensive schools and progressive teachers to reproduce the standards of the previous system amounted to a breakdown in cultural transmission and to a betrayal of the past. Schools were no longer able authoritatively to pass on a body of knowledge and standards of behaviour. Those who administered the schools, or who laid down or implemented curriculum policy, were to blame for an accelerating loss of cultural cohesion.

Teachers, headteachers and administrators were depicted as being instrumental in creating the decline in academic standards. The latter were measured largely in terms of basic literacy and numeracy skills as well as standards of behaviour. Not only were schools and teachers seen as lacking authority, they and the entire educational system were also seen to be largely unaccountable. Within a re-defined educational framework, it was envisaged that:

> From the centre, monitoring would be increased by a movement towards a standard curriculum for the majority of the syllabus, and by more vigilant work by the government inspectorate. From the local neighbourhood, parents would be given more say through a voucher scheme or through the publication of school results, allowing both for greater pressure on 'less successful' schools and for parental demand that their children should be transferred to schools of a higher standard. (CCCS, 1981: 206)

This theme, focused on surveillance of the school curriculum and teachers, was to assume a position of major importance in educational policy during the 1980s. The concepts of educational vouchers and payment-by-results advocated by Rhodes Boyson in the *Black Papers*, had their origin in the Report of the Newcastle Commission (1861) and the Revised Code (1862) (cf. Maclure, 1982). These meanings constructed around the notion of teacher accountability were to be reworked and subsequently feature again in the neo-Conservative discourse on improving educational standards during the 1980s.

The attack in the *Black Papers* on comprehensive education constituted as much a critique of the modernization project advocated by Vaizey and Harold Wilson as it did on concerns with 'equality of opportunity', 'disadvantage' and 'social justice' in the Newsom (1963) and Plowden Reports (1967). School success was judged largely in terms of selection, the ethos of hard work, traditional values and self-improvement which were seen as having provided the bedrock of the grammar school system. This perspective harked back romantically to a time when life was simple, more ordered and when talented working class children, like Rhodes Boyson, were given 'real' lifechances in the special opportunities offered to them to attend the selective grammar schools.

It was precisely this common-sense level of argument that contributed to the success of the *Black Papers* in getting public support. Their success derived from the fact that their discourse tied in with real concerns amongst many working-class parents and students who were not benefiting from the comprehensive school system (Jones, 1987). As is argued by Hall (1983: 38), the success of populist right-wing discourse:

> . . . does not lie in its capacity to dupe unsuspecting folk but in the way it addresses real problems, real and lived experiences, real contradictions – and yet is able to represent them within a logic of discourse which pulls them systematically in line with policies and class strategies of the right.

The perceived decline in educational standards in state education and, especially within the comprehensive school system, stood in stark juxtaposition with earlier possibilities of 'excellence' offered in the selective grammar school system. In offering open and equal access, the comprehensive ideal represented an exercise in increasing quantity at the expense of quality in education. The positive response amongst a cross-section of the population to the *Black Papers* reflected the basic lack of social consensus that surrounded the comprehensive education debate. What was taking place at a deeper level, was the emergence of new political forces organized around a populist discourse in which the contributors to the *Black Papers* and the media became the primary definers of what was relevant and important in education.

Fracturing the Comprehensive Education Discourse

Despite the central role that egalitarianism played in engendering the moral panic in the *Black Papers*, not much had changed with regard to educational practice within the new comprehensive system. Comprehensive education was highly fragmented and differentiated (Ball, 1981; Reynolds and Sullivan, 1987) and the drive for egalitarianism existed only in small pockets of innovation. According to Ball (1990: 31), 'the discourse of comprehensive education was a discourse of vagary, of uncertainty and of polarity, embracing as it did the extremes from the most radical to the most pragmatic'. Neither was there necessarily a common understanding amongst advocates of what comprehensive schools would mean in practice.

At one end of the spectrum there were those advocates for whom comprehensive education was grounded in egalitarian principles that required a complete re-imagining of the process of schooling. Thus it was argued that:

schools must exhibit a whole range of educational innovation and openness in the curriculum and teaching methods and relationships with the outside world which will bring about a new ethos and a new view of the child; only in a cooperative framework which sees children as of equal worth will equality be achieved. (Marsden, 1971: 22–23; quoted in Ball, 1981: 9)

This view of comprehensive schooling aspired to an extensive set of egalitarian ideals which would involve a fundamental process of systemic change supported further by affective and cultural transformation. In principle, this position underscored a socialist vision of socio-cultural change. At the other end, Anthony Crosland, Minister at the Department of Education and Science (DES) at the time maintained a belief in continued academic streaming, whereas for Harold Wilson the comprehensive ideal represented 'grammar schools for all' (Ball, 1981: 8). Thus the notion of the comprehensive school featured mainly as a rhetorical device in political speeches. These ambiguous meanings ultimately became inscribed into the resolution on comprehensive reorganization presented to parliament in 1965 and stated:

That this House, conscious of the need to raise educational standards at all levels, and regretting that the realisation of this objective is impeded by the separation of children into different types of secondary schools, notes with approval the efforts of local authorities to reorganise secondary education along comprehensive lines, which will preserve all that is valuable in grammar school education for those children who now receive it and make it available to more children; . . . and believes that the time is now ripe for a declaration of national policy. (quoted in Flew, 1994: 82)

This statement ratified the introduction of setting and streaming which were an intrinsic part of the grammar school, into the comprehensive school system. Open and universal access would be regulated by sifting mechanisms of quality control within the education system.

The fluidity in interpretations and understandings that featured in social discourse were reflected also at the level of practice. The wide range of interpretations contributed to the fact that the reorganization for comprehensive education lacked overall strategic coherence and solidarity amongst practitioners. In many areas the grammar school system remained intact, and in many comprehensive schools pupils were academically streamed, 'setted' and banded for particular subjects. Indeed, Ball (1981: 90) suggests that:

Most of the comprehensives created during the 1960s were probably of the meritocratic type, streamed academically and socially, and competing with grammar schools by entering large numbers of pupils for public examinations.

This highlights the fact that the comprehensive ideal that predominated at the time was essentially constituted in ambiguity, contradictions and tensions.

The *Black Papers* can be seen as having given voice to some of the various levels of discontent that surrounded comprehensive education as a policy initiative. Although the *Black Papers* did not have any immediate and direct impact on policy, the attention that they received in the media served an important political purpose in maintaining a critical focus on educational change and development during the 1960s, and well into the 1970s. Although the polemic was structured in terms of 'failing teachers', 'failing schools' and the need to improve 'standards in education', the notion of *effectiveness* did not yet feature as a variable. Rather, the emphasis was mainly on:

- the right of parents to have choice in selecting the schools that their children would attend;
- the intrinsic value and benefits of selective education (private) for those who could afford it;
- school discipline; a systematically ordered and regulated knowledge content, educational context and process;
- traditional teaching methods; and
- greater teacher and administrative accountability and efficiency.

Quality referred to the importance of the role of schools in inculcating traditional cultural values, self-improvement, teaching basic literacy and numeracy skills (the 3Rs) and a common curriculum framed by traditional subject knowledges.

The overall success of the *Black Papers* was the social construction of a 'crisis' in education necessitating state intervention in the organization and planning of the entire education process. A consensus was being shaped around a common-sense belief that 'something needed to be done'.

Education and the Needs of Industry

James Callaghan, then Labour Prime Minister, took up some of the themes in the *Black Papers* and also made links with some of the key issues identified in the modernization debate during the 1960s. Callaghan's speech at Ruskin College, Oxford (1976), has been heralded generally as having started the 'Great Debate' in, and about, education, and as representing the turning point in educational policy direction for the next two decades. It signified the beginnings of the process of legitimating increasing central government monitoring and later, during the 1980s, direct intervention in education. A new educational policy agenda was being forged.

Of significance were his concerns about progressive education, a major strand in the later *Black Papers*. Callaghan stated that:

There is the unease felt by parents and teachers about the new informal methods of teaching which seem to produce excellent results when they are in well-qualified hands but are much more dubious in their effects when they are not. (Ruskin College Speech, 1976)

Having canvassed the opinions of industry, Callaghan further argued that:

> I am concerned on my journeys to find complaints from industry that new recruits from the schools sometimes do not have the basic tools to do the job that is required . . . there is concern about the standards of numeracy of school leavers. (Ruskin College Speech, 1976)

This was a theme that had been articulated also in the media by prominent industrialists, supporting the argument that teachers needed to be accountable to parents and to industry. The focus on literacy and numeracy, a strand that also featured in the *Black Papers*, had by now been re-interpreted, reworked and inserted into another discourse centred on the levels of personal efficacy demanded by industry. Arguing that the two aims of education were 'to equip children to the best of their ability for a lively, constructive place in society and also to fit them to do a good job of work', Callaghan essentially linked personal efficacy with practical vocational training. He stated that 'there seems to be a need for more technological biases in science teaching that will lead towards applications in industry rather than towards academic studies' (Ruskin College Speech, 1976). On the surface, this supported both Vaizey's and Wilson's views during the 1960s on the necessary relationship between education and societal modernization.

However, in contrast to their arguments for increased levels of investment in education, the Ruskin College speech signified the beginnings of entirely new concerns around the need for a cost-effective educational system. Callaghan argued that:

> There has been a massive injection of resources to education, mainly to meet increased numbers and partly to raise standards. But in present circumstances, there can be little expectation of further increased resources being made available, at any rate for the time being. . . . There is a challenge to us all in these days and the challenge to education is to examine its priorities and to secure as high efficiency as possible by the skilful use of the £6 billion of existing resources. (Ruskin College Speech, 1976)

Allocating blame for the crisis in manufacturing industry, and, relatedly, the economy, to the failure of schools and teachers to produce adequate levels of literate and numerate proficiency, served an important political function. The high level of attention that the Ruskin College speech received in the media helped to divert attention away from the problems that existed between management, workers and trade unions at the time. CCCS (1981: 206) argue that 'the added voices of employers with their concern at allegedly declining standards of literacy and numeracy, served to clinch the political climate in which new forms of intervention became possible'. Four subjects for

Figure 2.1 Contributing factors to the economic crisis

- levels of unemployment rose as a result of low labour demands due to the effects of new technologies such as electronic printing, and the increased use of nuclear energy in some industries;
- high levels of unemployment due to the gradual erosion of the manufacturing base in the UK, and the export of production to regions with low labour costs such as South East Asia;
- rapid inflation, high levels of trade deficit, and increased Public Debt had necessitated the Government to borrow from the International Monetary Fund (IMF). The stringent controls tied in with these loans contributed to rising interest rates and a devalued currency;
- the failure of Labour's Social Contract with the trade unions, which was an agreement on controlled wage increases in return for policy concessions on employment and worker conditions, had led to a rising number of industrial disputes;
- the flight of investment capital to overseas markets as a result of the unstable currency situation and continuing labour disputes in the UK had led to a significant decrease in overseas investment in Britain.

discussion in the subsequent 'Great Debate' were identified. These included (a) the school curriculum 5–16, (b) the assessment of standards, (c) the education and training of teachers, and (d) school and working life. The Green Paper *Education in Schools: A Consultative Document* published in July 1977, called attention to national needs and underlined the centrality of school in meeting the needs of manufacturing industry.

Redefining Education

Themes from older, oppositional, discourses now became refracted and imbued with new sets of, largely, economistic meanings. The concepts of quality and effectiveness reconstructed within the context of the economic realities of the mid-1970s, implicitly, served to legitimate a redefined role for schooling and education. The deepening economic crisis of the mid- to late 1970s had several contributing factors. These are summarised in Figure 2.1.

Figure 2.1 shows the extent to which the economic difficulties that now predominated required state intervention. New solutions were necessary and this created the need for the state to restructure its economic management strategies in order to stimulate a by now stagnant economy. The themes identified in the Ruskin College speech, the 'Great Debate' and the subsequent Green Paper were essential elements in that process of restructuring. Following Callaghan's consultation with industry, education became an important focus for effecting specific forms of change. It became the context in which new economic and social awarenesses had to be shaped and realized as a necessary prerequisite for sustained economic growth.

The Ruskin College Speech managed to pull together what until now had been loose threads revolving around disciplinary interests, moral panics grounded in ideological prejudices and instinct, and which had been articulated within a variety of discourses. The Callaghan speech harnessed these discursive themes and gave them political coherence and legitimacy across what previously had been perceived to be an ideological divide between the political parties. Emphasis was beginning to shift from concerns about teachers' entitlements as workers/trade union members to:

- their professional accountability;
- their obligations and responsibilities to the nation;
- the economy and to parents;
- a need for structure and order, monitoring and control.

As is argued by Ball (1990: 31):

> Whatever Callaghan's intention the speech gave powerful encouragement and legitimacy to the 'discourse of derision' mounted by the *Black Papers*. In discursive terms it marked the end to any possibility of serious public opposition to the critique of comprehensivism and progressivism. It cleared the ground for a shift of emphasis on the Right from critical deconstruction to radical reconstruction.

The notion of *effectiveness* espoused in the Green Paper centred on making LEAs accountable for what was happening in schools with regard to curriculum provision, assessment and monitoring standards. The accountability of the DES to parliament was outlined, a central role was identified for the Secretaries of State in formulating a 'core' curriculum, and increased powers were given to the inspectorate to monitor curriculum provision. *Quality* was to be monitored in terms of pupils' levels of achievement, whilst teachers and teaching were to be subjected to external controls, which included a programme of national assessment conducted by the Assessment of Performance Unit (APU) set up in 1974 with the remit of monitoring standards in education.

Furthermore, the Taylor Committee (1977) in their report *A New Partnership for Our Schools*, spoke in favour of increasing the powers of school governing bodies. The new governing bodies would consist of an equal number of LEA representatives, parents, teachers, pupils (where appropriate) and members of the local community (Deem 1990: 154). Deem argues further that:

> The powers of the new bodies would include establishing the aims of the school and the ways in which these were to be achieved, although the headteacher would retain ultimate control. Other powers of governors would include submitting of annual estimates of school income and expenditure, consultation with the LEA over buildings and maintenance; joint responsibility with the LEA for appointment of heads and full responsibility for the appointment of other teachers. (Deem, 1990: 155)

The Taylor recommendations were only partially incorporated into the 1980 Education Act, and governors maintained only an advisory role (Deem, 1990).

What is significant to our analysis here is that, in an overall sense, key themes that had been articulated from a variety of ideological positions and defining sites during the preceding decade were now coming together in a new discourse centred on:

- raising educational standards;
- teachers' accountability to parents and the economy;
- parental choice; and
- a common curriculum.

These issues were subsequently to be incorporated into a different ideological framework and vision of education. Indeed, the whole terrain of educational debate and struggle was to be restructured within a new framework and new terms of reference both linguistically and conceptually. Systemic changes were to be put into effect demanding fundamental organizational as well as effective and cognitive adjustments to be made by teachers. A new era was emerging demanding new ways of seeing, new ways of knowing and new ways of 'doing' education.

Education and Market Principles

The Thatcher regime came to power in 1979 with an election manifesto promising radical solutions to the problems within the economy. Drawing on the ideological principles of the Austrian economist Friedrich Hayek, it placed the market at the centre of social policy. Stressing the need to maintain rigorous cash spending limits, it aimed to curb public expenditure by reducing the role of the state as both a key regulatory mechanism and manager of the economy. In Hayekian terms, state intervention in the economy was regarded as producing a 'politicized economy, which restricts competition and generates inflation' (Ball, 1990: 38). The market represented a neutral and rational regulatory mechanism; individual consumer choice exercised in the market would maximize productivity by creating new product demands. Other principles of this market-oriented ideology and their applications in the educational terrain will be discussed further in Chapter 4.

In keeping education as a topic on the popular agenda, the themes identified in the *Black Papers* had provided a 'common-sense' legitimacy to emergent neo-Conservative interests. Neo-Conservatism represented the views of a section in the party who drew on key themes in the *Black Papers*. Thus it was concerned mainly with the preservation of tradition, establishing and maintaining authority, excellence and standards in education. It supported the idea of streaming, formal teaching methods and formal tests as the basis of assessment. The attack on progressive education which initially had started in the *Black Papers*, gradually became incorporated into the overall neo-Conservative educational discourse. By the early 1980s it was being articulated from within newly established defining sites such as the Hillgate Group, the Centre for Policy Studies, the 'Salisbury Review' and the popular press. This polemic was aimed specifically at anti-racist teaching and multicultural education which they viewed as doctrinaire teaching and 'alien' to British culture. Another strand related to the removal of powers of control from Local Education Authorities (LEAs).

The neo-liberal element in the Conservative Party, on the other hand, represented the modernizers who, as Vaizey, Wilson and Callaghan in the Labour Party did earlier, supported the important link between education and economic growth. Primary concerns revolved around the value of competition in raising standards, and freedom of parental choice within the framework of the educational market. Inserting free-market principles of choice and competition into the educational system would increase accountability and efficiency. Articulating its desire to remove control from schools and LEAs within the framework of de-centralization, neo-liberal elements emphasized de-bureaucratization. This was to be achieved by the restructuring of the educational administrative system and the devolution of power to schools, and to parents as consumers.

The White Paper, *Better Schools* (1985) consolidated the requirements on school governance identified in the Education Act 1980. It provided an outline for the restructuring of school governance to 'define more clearly and establish more consistently the functions of these governing bodies' (DES, 1985: 63). The White Paper argued further that:

> If a school is to succeed in all its tasks, it needs to have an identity and a sense of purpose of its own. It needs to recognise itself more than an agency of the LEA. While the professionalism of its staff is a necessary condition for its success, it is not sufficient on its own. A school should serve the community from which it draws its pupils. (DES, 1985: 63)

Lay people, including parents from within the community were to be incorporated into the re-constituted governing body. It also recommended that 'appropriate powers for governing bodies should be entrenched by legislation so that these could not, as can happen at present, be overridden by the LEA' (DES, 1985: 64). The 1986 Education Act decreased LEA representation and increased co-opted community and business membership (Deem, 1990). More fundamental changes were to come with the 1988 Education Reform Act.

Raising Educational Standards and School Effectiveness

School effectiveness as a reference point of educational standards featured in Sir Keith Joseph's, then Secretary of State for Education, keynote address at the North of England Education Conference in 1984. Arguing that the English education system stood at a 'watershed' he stated that:

> This government's aim is to raise standards . . . achieving our aims – to develop the potential of every child and, as a nation, to prosper in a free and fully employed society depends much on the effectiveness of our schools. (Joseph, 1984)

Poor school management became an explanatory variable of declining educational standards:

> some schools, through weak management, display a lack of direction and even of order. Until this has been put right by resolute local action, it is impossible for pupils at the school to achieve even those standards which are now regarded as passable, let alone those to which we should aspire. (Joseph, 1984)

The focus on school effectiveness was maintained in the report *The Effects of Local Authority Expenditure Policies on Educational Provision in England, 1985*, published by the DES in 1986. Reporting the extent of the perceived deficiencies in the educational system it stated that:

> In over a quarter of the schools visited poor leadership and management at one or more levels was considered to be adversely affecting the quality of work, the levels and deployment of resources, the organisation and planning of the curriculum . . . and the morale of teachers. (DES, 1986, Paragraph 9.6)

Once again, important strands were coming together in what until now was a disparate and fragmented discourse, to map a new interpretational framework in which education was to be discussed. Keywords to feature in social discourse and educational debate from now on revolved around choice, standards, self-improvement, self-reliance and self-help. The first two derived from the neo-liberal framework whilst the last two featured very strongly in the anti-welfare ethos of neo-Conservativism. Of significance was the shift taking place from a macro-sociocultural perspective to a micro-focus on schools, teachers and their LEAs.

Educational change gained new impetus under Kenneth Baker, who became Secretary of State for Education in May 1986. Education was to be discussed increasingly within a corporate business framework, using the language of de-monopolization. The entire educational system was to be overhauled and restructured in the 1988 Education Reform Act (ERA), fundamentally altering the categories of description, forms of organization and modes of thinking about the educational process. Kenneth Baker speaking at the North of England Conference introduced the ERA as follows:

> It is about enhancing the life chances of young people. It is about devolution of authority and responsibility. It is about competition, choice and freedom . . . it is part of the search for – and achievement of – educational excellence. It is about quality and standards. (quoted in Deem, 1990: 156)

Within the ERA framework, the break-up of LEA control was effected in the financial delegation to schools under the Local Management of Schools Scheme (LMS), in which schools became responsible for the management of their own budgets. Parental choice was extended through the removal of restriction on the number of pupils that a school could enrol. In addition, schools were allowed to opt out of LEA control and become grant-maintained (GMS), subject to the outcome of parental voting.

The National Curriculum imposed a compulsory curriculum comprised of specified 'core' and 'foundation' subjects, which were to be framed by defined knowledge content and curriculum process in programmes of study. These in turn would be supported by assessment criteria provided by set attainment targets and levels of attainment at particular key stages which coincided with specific age-ranges, namely, 7, 11, 14 and 16. These were to serve as 'bench mark' assessments. Other changes included the setting up of links with industry, business partnerships, the appraisal of teachers, and the specification of the number of annual directed teaching hours. The reshaping of governing bodies was represented as 'transferring power from producers to consumers and about making schools more "effective"' (Deem, 1990: 160).

As part of the implementation of the National Curriculum, schools were required to produce National Development Plans or School Development Plans under the management and advice of LEAs. These development plans were 'to be based on a systematic review of the changes needed in the curriculum, organization, and use of resources in their schools' (DES, 17 February 1989a) and would form the basis of bids for financial support under the Educational Support Grant (ESG) scheme or the Local Educational Authority Training Grants Scheme (LEATGS).

New Forms of Control

As an important management tool, the school development plans needed to be based on the school's curriculum policy, curriculum aims, and an outline of existing whole curriculum provision as well as assessment and reporting policies. They also needed to outline resource management such as accommodation, books, materials and equipment. It also included human resource management centred on in-service training 'to enhance staff expertise' with regard to the implementation of the National Curriculum and the development of subject expertises. Schools needed to identify their development priorities and provide time scales for change to be effected (DES, 17 February, 1989a).

Furthermore, *DES Circular 14/89* provided an outline of the regulations to guide schools in the implementation of the 1988 ERA, and section 8 of the 1980 Education Act. The *Circular* focused mainly on the information needs of various people involved at different levels in education including parents, governing bodies, pupils, headteachers, LEAs, HMI, the National Curriculum

Council (NCC), the School Examination and Assessment Council (SEAC) and the DES. Schools now were required to produce a school prospectus which contained information about their governing body's curriculum policy, curriculum aims, information on National Curriculum provision for specific year groups, career education, and information about 'how to make a complaint under section 23 of ERA' (DES 1989b: 7). This echoed the 1985 White Paper *Better Schools*, which advocated the need for schools to have their own identity and a sense of purpose. A corporate business model of management with schools having their own logo and mission statement thus emerged to provide the practical and ideological basis of educational change and development for the new millennium (see Chapter 5).

Headteachers were to make available published HMI reports related to the school, schemes of work used, the syllabus for RE, arrangements for sex education and information about pupils with special educational needs for whom the National Curriculum had been disapplied or modified. Schools were required also to make detailed 'annual returns of their whole curriculum, showing the place of the National Curriculum within it' (DES, 14/89). What is significant is the extent to which the focus had shifted to schools and their accountability to parents as consumers of educational services. The whole system and process of education were further subjected to surveillance by central forces in education such as the Department of Education and Science (DES), later to be reconstituted as the Department for Education and Employment (DfEE), Her Majesty's Inspectorate (HMI) which were to become OFSTED, and the School Examination and Assessment Council (SEAC) which was to become School Curriculum and Assessment Agency (SCAA). The latter has now merged with the National Council for Vocational Qualifications (NCVQ) to become the Qualifications and Curriculum Authority (QCA).

Summary

The chapter used as its starting point the 1960s as the period during which the relationship between education and economic development, and parallel concerns about standards in education first entered professional and policy debate.

1 It examined the ideological and social meanings attached to the notions of quality and effectiveness in social discourse during that time. This discussion was linked with broader events and developments within the social terrain and the ways in which these served to legitimate preferred sets of meanings over other, competing, perspectives.
2 Charting the post-ERA trajectory of educational change and development, it examined the particular model of success that underpins contemporary notions of the 'successful' school.

3   Drawing on key themes and motifs identified in earlier discourses, it highlighted continuities and discontinuities in the ongoing debate about the role of education and schooling in society.

4   It looked at the model of educational change that is underwritten in the 1988 Educational Reform Act and highlighted its influence on the emergence of particular organizational and management practices that now feature in many schools.

The decade that followed the 1988 Education Reform Act witnessed some of the most fundamental and far-reaching systemic, structural, ideological and cultural changes in education in England and Wales this century. Education during the entire 1980s had become a primary signifier of social and educational change. It has continued to be a profoundly politicized arena in which a variety of ideological and political agendas have been played out. Restructuring the role of teachers and redefining the power base of LEAs were to provide key elements around which consensus could be reached within a deeply ideologically divided Conservative Government during the 1980s and for most of the 1990s. The latter refers to the tensions that prevailed between the neo-liberal and the neo-Conservative elements within the Conservative Government.

Within the political climate of the time, fundamental changes were taking place in the whole social ethos. For example, the Thatcher government's sustained attack on trade union power resulted in shifting the parameters of political possibilities mainly in support of capital interests. This was to have a ripple effect on developments within the public services as a whole, including education. The 'discursive reworking of the parameters of political possibility and acceptability' (Ball, 1990: 38) within and through government policy, with the tacit support of defining agents such as the media, had altered the entire terrain of both social and educational struggle.

Ten years after ERA, we find teachers not as cultural workers able to engage freely in critique and self-definition, creating new spaces within which the parameters of educational debate and pedagogical possibility could be redefined. Instead, we find them rigidly locked into the technicism of school effectiveness taxonomies focused on quality control which, in turn, are subjected to a myriad of external and internal bureaucratic forms of control (see also Chapter 4). In contrast to Plowden's (1967) perspective, that at the heart of the education process lies the child, emphasis has shifted qualitatively towards concerns about the *effectiveness* of schools and the *performativity* of teachers. Circumscribed by centrally defined, standardized sets of measurable criteria, the notion of school effectiveness framed by the Education Reform Act (ERA) (1988) in England and Wales, has focused on:

- narrowly defined professional competencies;
- the regulation of task-oriented institutional practices and processes, systems monitoring and the management of, largely, attitudinal and behavioural change within organizations.

School *performance* now represents the central concern within an education system penetrated by a cascade of over-regulation.

Theorizations shaped around 'performativity' and work process exclude analysis of societal relations and asymmetries of power within the educational system. These have presented an apolitical, ahistorical and de-ideologized view of educational change and development. Whilst much has been written about the process-management of organizational change, not much has been said in general educational discussion about the overall development of education as a socio-cultural practice. The culture of management that now frames educational policy and practice, and the predominant focus on the monitoring of work practices and processes, have dislocated education from its socio-cultural base.

Questions

1 Identify some of the key influences in the movement to raise educational standards.
2 What were the four main subjects for discussion in the Great Debate?
3 What, in your view, are the essential ingredients of an effective school?
4 To what extent do the principles on comprehensive education, and the child-centred learning advocated in the Plowden Report still prevail in contemporary education?
5 To what extent have the principles of 'a good education' identified in the 'Great Debate' been fulfilled in the 1988 Education Reform Act?

Chapter 3

Towards the Japanization of Education in England and Wales

As we saw in Chapters 1 and 2, discursive influences within the social and educational terrain impacted in different ways on the general debate about the role of education in society during the 1960s and 1970s. Continuing that discussion, we explore one of the main arguments of the book, namely, that educational policy and research cannot be decontextualized from society, politics and culture. We argue that the ascendancy of school effectiveness in national educational policy reflects ongoing management concerns within the state. Drawing on French regulation theory (Aglietta, 1979; Lipietz, 1979, De Vroey, 1984), the chapter seeks to highlight the relationship between concerns about accountability, effectiveness, efficiency and economy in the educational system and:

- the ongoing restructuring of the capital accumulation process (i.e. the systematized means by which capital profits are generated);
- the transition from an industrial-based economy to the multifaceted technologically-driven capital accumulation process; and
- the emergence of a new capitalist mode of regulation.

Within the analytic framework of regulation theory, the *mode of regulation* refers to:

> the ensemblement of the institutional forms, networks and explicit or implicit norms which assure compatibility of market behaviour within a regime of accumulation, in keeping with the actual pattern of social relations, and beyond (or even through) the contradictory, conflictual nature of relations among economic agents and social groups. (Bonefeld, 1987: 99–100)

Discursively constructed, and organic in the way in which it operates, the mode of regulation serves to secure hegemonic, structural and system support for the overall capital accumulation process. Hegemony refers to the rationalization of:

> relations of domination and subordination, in their forms as practical consciousness, as in effect a saturation of the whole process of living – to such a depth that the pressures and limits of what can ultimately be seen as a specific economic, political and cultural system seem to most of us the pressures and limits of simple experience and common sense. (Williams, 1989: 57)

We argue that school effectiveness represents a potent political and rhetorical device through which education can be incorporated into the overall re-structuring of economic and societal relations during a period of sustained economic crisis and social change. We focus, in particular, on the emergence of new organizational forms as an integral part of the structural and systemic changes that have evolved in the UK economy during the 1980s. *Organizational forms* describe the strategic ways in which social, economic and political institutions, processes and practices have been reconstituted as part of the process of national and global economic crisis management. *Structural changes* refer to the evolution of new forms of production, the re-organization of work practices, of labour and labour relations, and the restructuring of the capital accumulation process. Together these support the development of a new mode of regulation. *Systemic change* refers to the transition from one socio-cultural, technological, political and economic milieu to another, and overall transformations within the global cultural economy.

This discussion prepares the context for a critical exploration of the interactive relationship that exists between post-ERA concerns about school effectiveness, and the analytic categories and terms of reference that frame economics and labour management theories. An underlying argument is that the market systems and quality control practices and processes put into place in schools, and the education system as a whole, form an integral part of the general management of the ongoing economic crisis. We argue that the emphasis on teacher accountability transfers the onus for effective schooling onto teachers whilst allocating a primarily regulatory and monitoring role to the state. In restructuring the educational system as a whole, neo-liberal (and now reinforced by New Labour) policy meanings have redefined not only the educational process, but also teachers' consciousness as workers, and the expectations and role of parents as consumers. In thus securing hegemonic support, the structural and systemic changes taking place within education can be seen as forming an important part of the new mode of (free-market) capitalist regulation.

Represented as 'modern' policies to suit a 'modern' economy within a 'modernizing' social milieu, educational policy initiatives, at least during the past decade, have occupied a key position in the restructuring process. Signifying a potent form of hegemonic cultural capital (i.e. that to which we all must adapt) these policy interventions are aimed at providing stability to the new regime of accumulation. Within the framework of regulation theory, the term 'regime of accumulation' refers to 'the specific institutional framework and social norms proper to various stages of capitalist development' (De Vroey, 1984: 52). This includes not only the re-composition of the labour force, and the restructuring of the labour process and commodity relations, but also a reshaping of worker consciousness. We will examine these issues within the context of the debate about the transition from Fordism to 'post-Fordism'.

The Crisis of Fordism

As we saw in Chapter 2, by the late 1970s a consensus was emerging around the view that high levels of investment in education, supported by the principles of human capital theory, had not yielded the expected social and economic returns. Already by the time of the last Black Paper (1975), and Callaghan's Ruskin College Speech (1976), education was seen as not having fulfilled its promise to society. The education system was seen as highly bureaucratized with LEAs, teachers and their trade unions wielding disproportionate levels of power. Indeed, by the time that the Conservative Government came to power in 1979:

> Education had come to epitomize much that was seen to be wrong with burgeoning state power. It was construed as expensive, not self-evidently adequately productive, insufficiently accountable, monopolistic, producer-dominated, a bastion of an entrenched professional elite, resistant to consumer demand and, at worst, self-generating and self-serving. (Fergusson, 1996: 93)

These meanings circulating in various discourses throughout the 1970s and 1980s, derived legitimacy to a large extent from the parlous state of the economy at the time. In Britain the economic crisis revolved around:

1   Stagnant markets.
2   Low levels of productivity in the manufacturing sector.
3   High levels of unemployment.
4   Lack of investment in the development of new products, and relatedly,
5   Britain's inability to compete successfully in an increasingly globalized economy.

Together, these difficulties within the economy contributed to a general reduction in the Gross Domestic Product (GDP). Harvey (1989: 142) ascribes this to the fact that:

> There were problems of rigidities in labour markets, labour allocation, and in labour contracts (especially in the so-called 'monopoly' sector). And any attempt to overcome these rigidities ran into the seemingly immovable force of deeply entrenched working-class power ... The rigidities of state commitments also became more serious as entitlement programmes (social security, pension rights etc.) grew under pressure to keep legitimacy at a time when rigidities in production restricted any expansion in the fiscal basis for state expenditures.

Greater demands, made by workers, on the public purse could no longer be sustained. The rigidities referred to here have been attributed generally to the structural limitations of what has been referred to as the Fordist mode of production oriented towards standardized mass consumption.

The Fordist production process used in the post-War manufacturing industry, and particularly in the car manufacturing industry during the 1950s and 1960s, was typified by clear job demarcation and task/job fragmentation in the semi-automatic assembly-line. That is to say, workers were not engaged in completing work tasks in their entirety. Instead, individual workers were responsible for task performance on one component of the overall production of, for example, an artefact. The Fordist production process also relied on strong forms of supervised control with work stoppages such as shift transfer, coffee/tea/lunch breaks forming an integral part of the regulation of the working day. During the economic crisis of the 1970s, interruptions in the working day became increasingly seen as not being cost-effective with regard to both time-management and product throughput. Productivity would be improved by reducing the number of gaps in the working day. The overall rigidity of the Fordist production process presented difficulties in terms of responding quickly to new production demands within the market place.

Within the broader economy, the need for increased levels of inward investment, and the imperative to boost export meant that the country had to become more competitive within an international market place dominated by the capital markets of Japan, the USA – and increasing competition from the then burgeoning 'tiger' economies in the Pacific Rim. Managing the economic crisis thus necessitated complex restructuring, some of which involved the adoption of new organizational forms and structural change.

Economic Management and The Restructuring of Capital

The Conservative Government's adoption of a neo-liberal economic policy approach based on free enterprise, free trade, and the deregulation of money markets provided the ideological basis for the modernization of the economy (Lipietz, 1994). According to the logic of neo-liberalism, placing the market as the key regulatory mechanism at the centre of its economic policy strategy, deregulating financial markets and facilitating capital transfer would free capital and, in the process, stimulate the development of flexible capital accumulation strategies. The introduction of information technology during the 1980s into banking systems, currency markets and stock exchanges aided international capital transfer and heralded the rise of finance capital as a pivotal element in the restructuring of the capital accumulation process. Its incorporation into various industries throughout the 1980s transformed the production process and forms of work organization, placing a sharp emphasis on entrepreneurism and innovation. Structural changes effected within the restructured economy are summarized in Figure 3.1.

The imperative for education as a whole to adjust to the changes taking place in the economy identified in Figure 3.1, had been underscored within defining sites such as the Organization for Economic Co-operation and

Figure 3.1:   Key aspects of economic restructuring

- global shifts in the patterns of consumption;
- new forms of production;
- re-organization of work practices;
- re-organization of labour and labour relations;
- restructuring of capital accumulation strategies;
- new mode of regulation.

Development (OECD). In 1989, the OECD provided a new vision on the relationship between education and the state of the economy. It argued that:

> In the midst of the change and uncertainty that are sweeping OECD econom-
> ies, 'education and the economy' has become a catch-phrase for a vague
> but urgent dissatisfaction with the *status quo*. It does not proceed from
> well-articulated ideas of what the two – education, the economy – have to
> do with one another or what direction policy changes should take. *Rather it
> is motivated by inescapable evidence that the OECD economies are changing
> in unprecedented and unpredictable ways.* (OECD, 1989a: 3, emphasis added)

Of significance to education were the changes that were taking place in different sectors of the economy. The most marked transformation during the 1980s was the shift from manufacturing to the service sector (Massey and Allen, 1992). This, in turn, effected structural changes in the labour market, with more people entering employment in banks, insurance, real estate, healthcare, shops, restaurants and the leisure industry rather than factories. Central to this shift in the labour market was the gendering of employment with a general increase in, part-time, female employment. The changes that were now taking place in the labour market impacted on skills training needs in, for example, business management and other job-specific skills requiring specialist short-term training, some of which were predominantly information-based.

Of greater significance was the deepening of the crisis in the manufacturing sector of the economy. Whilst the financial and service sectors were buoyant, manufacturing industry remained in crisis with the country having the largest trade deficit in manufacturing goods since the war (Avis et al., 1996). Concern about British industry's lack of competitiveness led to the publication of a report in 1991 by The House of Lords Select Committee on Science and Technology. The report, *Innovation in Manufacturing Industry*, stated that:

> The failure of British manufacturing industry to remain competitive has had
> serious consequences. Our manufacturing base has declined. Our home
> market is increasingly penetrated by imports. Our share of world markets in
> manufactured goods is too small. The implications for our future prosperity
> are grave . . . The small size of the manufacturing base will constrain the
> growth in output which we need in the future. Only a substantial increase
> in output can correct the huge deficit in our balance of trade, without

decline in the quality of life in the United Kingdom . . . When the economy expands again and demand increases, the deficit will grow again unless industry becomes more competitive and so increases profitable sales. (quoted in Avis et al., 1996: 55–56)

Some of the difficulties encountered in the manufacturing industry were attributed to the high cost of labour maintenance and labour management. Others were related more directly to stagnant markets and commodity production. The generalized difficulties in the economy referred to above have been ascribed implicitly to the crisis of the Fordist mode of production, regulation and accumulation.

The Transition from 'Fordism' to the 'Flexible' Firm

In order to regain a competitive edge within an increasingly technologically driven global market, business and industry required higher levels of investment in information technology as well as increased opportunities for innovation and enterprise development. Britain lacked investment in large high-tech industries with 'high investment in research and development, and a substantial science base' (Avis et al., 1996: 56). These factors impacted on possibilities for innovation and product development to meet ever-changing market demands for new, customized products catering for increasingly more discerning consumer choice within a highly differentiated international consumer market. Technologically-driven innovation, research and development, and the re-organization of labour and labour relations became imperative if British manufacturing industry were to become more competitive within the global market. According to Harvey (1989: 155):

in many instances competitive pressures and the struggle for better labour control led either to the rise of entirely new industrial forms or to the integration of Fordism with a whole network of subcontracting and 'outsourcing' to give greater flexibility in the face of competition and greater risk.

New hybrid, flexible organizational forms influenced by industrial work practices elsewhere were beginning to emerge in the UK workplace to make production more cost-effective and efficient in order to increase productivity. These are discussed below.

Corporate Restructuring

Corporate response throughout the 1980s centred largely on investment in:

- the development of their technological infrastructure;
- creating new product lines (diversification);

- generating new markets by creating new product niches;
- resource rationalization (decreasing staffing through redundancies, early retirement packages, part-time and fixed-term employment);
- restructuring (including mergers); and
- de-monopolization.

The underlying aim was to increase market competition and, relatedly, to be able to respond more quickly and effectively to international competition. Resource management focused predominantly on facilitating cost-effective, 'lean' production and human resource development.

Companies were also increasingly looking towards Japan as an exemplary model of both worker and production management. Bratton (1992: 22) states that:

> It is the competitiveness of such companies as Hitachi, Matsushita, Nissan, Sanyo, Toyota and others that has intrigued British and North American industrial managers, and compelled them to look to Japanese management practices as a role model and catalyst which would cause a resurgence of innovation and renewal.

The integration of some of these organizational changes into business corporations were to have a major impact on the various ways in which schools re-organized themselves to accommodate the requirements of the 1988 Education Reform Act. In order to contextualize the organizational changes that have taken place within schools, and their association with prevailing notions of school effectiveness, we will first take a detailed look at Japanese production practices, processes and labour management. In particular, we will examine the ideology that underpinned the Japanese business management model. Alongside this we will also look at the Total Quality Management (TQM) ideology that has underpinned work and management practices in the US during the past two decades.

Japanese Work Practices and Business Ideology

According to Imai (1986) the key to the overall success of Japanese business and industry lies first in the philosophical concept of *kaizen* which, he argues, provides the best means by which all aspects of Japanese production and management can be understood. *Kaizen*, literally translated, means continuous improvement 'involving everyone, including both managers and workers' (Imai, 1986: 3). It is a generic term which penetrates all aspects of Japanese life. Imai (1986: 3) states that '(t)he *kaizen* philosophy assumes that our way of life – be it our working life, our social life, or our home life – deserves to be constantly improved'. We can therefore say that the concept of *kaizen* is imbued with a work ethic or work preparedness grounded in self-monitoring. *Kaizen* forms an integral part of the Japanese 'social character'. Raymond Williams (1961: 63) describes the social character as 'a valued system of behaviour and attitudes (that) is taught formally and informally . . . a selection and configuration of interests and activities, and a particular valuation of them, producing a distinct organisation, a "way of life"'. As such, *kaizen* can be seen as constituting hegemonic cultural capital; it provides a significant cultural means by which the Japanese 'way of life' is produced and reproduced.

The concept of 'companyism' or *kaisha* provides a second key organizing principle of Japanese work culture. *Kaisha* is ideological and can best be described as a set of rules, company (and tacit) beliefs, expectations, behaviours and procedures through which workers are incorporated into the firm's culture (Yoshimura and Anderson, 1997). These include loyalty to the firm in every respect and also extend to family life. In return, the firm offers on-the-job training, lifetime employment (which, in economic terms, is off-set against the fact that it serves to prevent losing the returns of their investment in workers' training, and reducing the need for constant training of new staff), treating workers of equivalent competence equally, seniority-based promotion and 'the use of variable bonuses to give firms wage flexibility' (Banno, 1997: 182).

Framed by the ideological principles of both *kaizen* and *kaisha*, the Japanese production model is centred on co-operative team work, flexible job demarcation (workers are expected to switch tasks frequently and thus need to be multi-skilled) and flexible forms of work organization. These, and the TQM practices in US work organizations, are summarized below:

- 'lean production' made up of small production units;
- 'just-in-time' (JIT) strategies form part of total quality control and involve small batch production which circumvents the need for stock-piling and the keeping of inventories, and thus reduces waste whilst at the same time maintaining total quality control. JIT aims at eliminating overproduction, time wasted at the machine, 'waste involved in the transportation of units, waste in processing, waste in taking inventory, waste of motion, and waste in the form of defective units' (Imai, 1986: 89);
- cellular technology (CT) – involves: grouping together a configuration of machine tools for the production of a 'family' of similar components, rather than by function. All operations on a given component are performed in a U-shaped line or cell which reduces work-in progress and increases the throughput of work by simplifying the flow. A cellular work structure forms new work groups. The specialized skilled machinist operating one machine tool, in one particular work station, is replaced by a generalized skilled machinist with flexible job boundaries (Bratton, 1992: 23). Cellular manufacturing is flexible in that the size of the group can be re-constituted according to the requirements of specific jobs. Its physical organization encourages

workers to co-operate and to engage in problem-solving and quality improvement (Bratton, 1992). The function of CT is to facilitate task-management in the production process;

- quality circles (QCs) – constitute small groups of workers that perform a continuous quality control function. The emphasis in quality circles is on 'self-development, mutual education, and flow control and improvement within the workshop' (Imai, 1986: 11). QCs represent multi-skilled labour management aimed at improving the phases of production for which they are responsible. As part of the process, workers and managers are consulted and problems of production and management are discussed and eliminated (Piore and Sabel, 1984);

- total quality control (TQC) – commitment to 'zero-defect', 'every process is controlled by monitoring the quality during production' resulting in an overall decrease in labour costs and material wastage (Bratton, 1992: 27). TQC spans the whole production process including research, design, product development and technology. Within each work component it covers a broad area including quality assurance, cost reduction, meeting production quotas and delivery schedules, safety, new product development, productivity improvement and supplier management (JIT);

- total quality management (TQM) used in US industry refers to company-wide continuous improvement as part of the process of overall quality control. In Japan it operates through self-surveillance and 'Neighbour Check' monitoring embedded in *kaizen*;

- integrated, horizontally organized work teams engaged in task-oriented, face-to-face interaction, allowing them to consult each other as an integral part of the production process;

- company-based trade unions engaged in consensus decision-making – forming part of human resource management policy and within this framework, 'enterprise unions tend to develop "company consciousness" rather than "union consciousness"' (Bratton, 1992: 30).

Through the work practices and processes described here workers gain information about new ways of doing the job and solving problems, 'best knowledge of work routines' and in *kaizen* meetings make suggestions for improvement to the company (Garrahan and Stewart, 1992: 75). In turn, the performance of supervisors is measured in terms of the number of workers' suggestions offered, and the manager of the 'supervisors is expected to assist them so that they can help workers generate more suggestions' (Imai, 1986: 15). The overall emphasis is on *process*, and concerns or problems in the work process are evaluated according to the following criteria:

- discipline;
- time management;
- skill development;

- participation and involvement;
- morale; and
- communication.

Together these different aspects extend to worker appraisal, task-oriented worker awarenesses, and employee participation in decision making. Thus workers are incorporated conceptually, psychologically and physically into the culture of the workplace, and subjected further to the totalizing 'gaze' of task, self- and external monitoring.

Japanese work practices were imported into different sectors of British manufacturing production – and at first – in the car manufacturing industry. During the early 1980s, many Japanese corporations such as Nissan, Toyota, and Honda exported their production plants to countries such as the USA and Britain, altering work practices and the culture of organizations from within.

From Fordism to 'Post-Fordism' – or to 'Neo-Fordism'?

Interpretations of the nature of the changes that have taken place in work organizations in the UK vary. Some argue that the emergence of new flexible capital accumulation strategies and production regimes herald a 'new historical bloc' which signifies a definitive end to the crisis of Fordist mass production (Bonefeld, 1987; Harvey, 1989). According to such theorizations information technology has contributed to the fact that we are moving towards a post-Fordist, technological mode of production. Computer-aided design and manufacture (CAD/CAM) which enable the integration of flexible forms of labour, it is suggested, has contributed to increased levels of productivity. Moreover, new flexible work practices including co-operative, integrated team work which involves a horizontal dispersal of control within the production process, are viewed by many as being potentially enabling to craft labour (Piore and Sabel, 1984). Flexible specialization, according to this view, enables labour to free itself from capital.

However, critiques of the post-Fordist thesis suggest that, in practice, the notions of worker and skills flexibility have effectively eroded workers' relative levels of control over the production process (Pollert, 1988; Tomaney, 1994). Indeed, it is argued that flexible work processes relying on worker efficiency, high levels of worker motivation, and task-orientation have contributed to an increase in self-monitoring, and the intensification of work. New production regimes and the forms of worker control in which they are embedded – combined with the exigencies of the market – have contributed to 'intermittent employment amongst periphery workers and a steady rise in non-unionised, low wage labour' (Rassool, 1993: 229–230). Thus they have eroded the notion of job security.

Within this framework, the notion of employability is underscored by:

- positive attitudes to change;
- worker and skills flexibility;
- the motivation to work;
- the ability of workers to adapt rapidly to change; and
- rational self-management.

Thus the onus for employment is transferred to the individual worker and her/his adaptability and willingness to change. The implication is therefore that instead of allusions to the labour-enhancing attributes of the post-Fordist work process, in practice, workplace flexibility shares more commonalities with the concept of 'neo-Fordism' or 'neo-Taylorism'. The latter concept derives from the mechanized industrial work practices supported by Frederick Taylor during the early part of this century in which productivity was measured in time-and-motion studies with the ultimate aim of reducing gaps in the working day. According to Sabel (1984: 236):

> Taylor's idea was for management to secure the most efficient possible use of labor by codifying craft knowledge and deciding by scientific means the one right way to do a particular job. Workers were then to be forced to execute this plan exactly through the promise of high wages and the threat of sanctions for disobedience.

Taylorism ensured the reduction of worker autonomy over the labour process placing them 'under a permanent surveillance and control in the fulfilment of their output norm' (Aglietta, 1979: 114).

Analyses of social, economic and cultural change located within these theoretical frameworks have generated much debate with regard to the actual changes that have emerged within a variety of countries, each having different social, economic, political and cultural bases. Amongst other arguments, there are disagreements about 'whether the shift from Fordism to post-Fordism offers an adequate description of current organisational and economic trends' (Brown and Lauder, 1992: 3). These writers maintain further that in many of the writings within the field:

> The description of a shift from Fordism to post-Fordism is obviously presented in ideal-typical terms, and as a consequence it tends to highlight change rather than continuity. It also tends to assume that countries can be characterized in terms of one or the other. (Brown and Lauder, 1992: 3)

How realistically then can we talk about definitive shifts having taken place from 'Fordism' to 'post-Fordism' or 'neo-Fordism'? To what extent do existing local conditions influence the type and nature of the changes that can, and do take place within different societies?

The rest of the chapter charts the formative influences of developments within the social and economic terrain, on the evolution of the work practices and forms of organization that have evolved within schools and which support a particular model of educational change and development. We look at influences from key theories within the rapidly growing school effectiveness industry on various work and quality management systems and practices that are evolving in schools. We provide a critical analysis of the mismatches and contradictions that exist between the normative terms of reference, the rigidity and technicism that frame the school effectiveness paradigm, and the parallel concepts of workplace flexibility and professional empowerment associated with the notion of school improvement. Normative terms of reference here refer specifically to the widespread use of taxonomies which frame standardized achievements, attainments and efficiencies in the measurement of school effectiveness. Gaps and silences in school effectiveness discourses on issues of societal and institutional power imbalances, and their impact on the overall experience of education, are highlighted. These are juxtaposed with considerations of cultural power and equity. Comparisons between the ideological meanings that pervaded neo-liberal underpinnings of educational change and development are juxtaposed throughout with those emerging within the framework of New Labour social policy.

Corporate Influences on Educational Change and Development

The centrality of educational reform to the political project of successive Conservative governments throughout the 1980s and most of the 1990s, gives an indication of the high level of priority accorded to the modernization of the educational system. A key underscoring principle was the imperative 'to prepare pupils to meet the needs of the 21st century' (DES, 1989d: 1). Thus, as we argued earlier, it served the purpose of bringing education in line with perceived changing economic realities, especially the need in the labour market for:

- increased worker efficiency;
- an awareness of cost-effective production, enterprise and innovation;
- the need to generate an understanding of global markets; and
- to raise productivity levels in order to increase Britain's competitive edge in the global market economy.

The meanings espoused within the Conservative policy framework have been continued within the New Labour educational policy agenda. With many of the systemic and structural changes following the 1988 ERA now in place, New Labour policy initiatives in education so far have focused on raising standards in education by 'encouraging best practice and effective monitoring with speedy intervention where necessary' (DfEE, 1997: 11). The White Paper, *Excellence in Schools* (1997), supporting the principles of the 1988 ERA, overtly links ongoing educational change and development with evolving needs in the economy within the broader framework of global capital markets. Placing education at the heart of government, the White Paper states that:

> We face new challenges at home and from international competitors, such as the Pacific Rim countries. They do not rely on market forces alone in education and neither should we. It is time now to get to the heart of raising standards – improving the quality of teaching and learning. (DfEE, 1997: 11)

The White Paper (DfEE, 1997) further emphasizes the shift in skills and knowledge need within the new technological society. It argues that:

> Investment in learning in the 21st century is the equivalent of investment in the machinery and technical innovation that was essential to the first great industrial revolution. Then it was capital; now it is human capital. We need to build up the store of knowledge and keep abreast of technological development if we are to prepare the future generation. (DfEE, 1997: 15)

The emphasis now has shifted to human resource development (HRD). Human capital theory now features within a different policy agenda to that which framed societal modernization during the 1950s and 1960s. Within the projected knowledge-based society of the new millennium the accent is on developing excellence grounded in the ideal of the *learning society*. The latter is seen as committed to continuous learning throughout life and 'the pursuit of quality and a commitment to high standards' (Dearing, 1995: 1). In practice, the ideal of a learning society has a dual meaning. First, it implies a society that evaluates, and learns about itself reflexively. Second, it implies a society that values education throughout one's lifetime, and for a variety of purposes. However, within the current educational policy framework, the concept of the 'learning society' takes on meanings specifically oriented towards a decontextualized and content-less process of continuous learning and skills development, self-monitoring and quality management. Economies of scale reflected in increased investment in education during the 1960s and 1970s now have been replaced by economies of scope with a sharp focus on capacity building grounded qualitatively in the notion of organizational and managerial effectiveness.

Many of these meanings were supported within influential contexts such as the OECD, which argued that economic restructuring needed to encompass a great deal more than the adjustment of fiscal and monetary policy. The OECD (1989a) advocated the need for adjustments to be made at micro-economic level as well as in institutional dynamics in order for education to be able to respond adequately to rapid shifts in skills and qualifications requirements in the labour market. According to the OECD (1989a: 18) 'this requires not just government intervention, but the consensus and concerted participation of employers, trade unions, producers, and consumers'. Taking account of economic restructuring and the resultant changes taking place within the labour process and the labour market discussed above, the OECD view can be seen as supporting the need to create the conditions necessary to support a new regime of accumulation within a new mode of capitalist regulation.

Whereas the overall emphasis in Conservative policy in education was on marketization, New Labour's educational project has consolidated the principles of *quality* and *excellence* in schools. The latter is based to a large extent on a competitive and normative view of school performance. The White Paper *Excellence in Schools*, states that:

> effective change in a field as dependent on human interaction as education requires millions of people to *change their behaviour*. That will require consistent advocacy and persuasion to create a climate in which schools are *constantly challenged to compare themselves to other similar schools and adopt ways of raising their performance*. (HMSO, 1997: 12, emphasis added)

This 'benchmarking' reduces educational change to a taken-for-granted changing of behaviours. These behaviours are embedded in the continuous improvement emphasis of *kaizen* and thus forms an integral part of a competitive market ideology (see also school improvement in Chapter 5). There are no indications of the nature of educational development beyond concerns about measurable 'performativities' and attitudinal changes. As we argued in Chapter 1, this positivistic view of educational change and development relies predominantly on quantitative data as a basis for policy decision making. At the level of consciousness, it engages schools in the totalizing process of self-monitoring and self-correction reflected in the neo-Taylorist work process described above. Intensification of the labour process within schools has contributed to emphases having shifted away from the affective and aesthetic elements of education to a primary concern with cognate institutional rationalities and performances.

The predominant focus on comparative levels of institutional performance does not overtly, or inherently, address issues related to difference, complexity and inclusion, and peripheralization. In providing a homogenized view of schools as neutral educational production sites, this micro-contextual approach does not engage *per se* with issues of 'how individuals learn, how knowledge is produced, and how subject positions are constructed' (Giroux, 1992: 81) within and through the educational system. Nor does it provide the scope to address the relationship between subjective organizational and societal factors. By focusing only on what is going on *in* schools, it represents a 'closed system' view of the world (Peters and Waterman, 1995: 91). In this sense then, the concept of excellence in schools that now features in the New Labour educational policy framework, in effect, consolidates the technical-rational approach that framed the market-orientation of Conservative education policy. Here the emphasis is on measurable quality product throughput.

In order to explore this further, the next section will focus on key aspects of educational policy since 1988 and the role that they played in putting in place the systems, processes and practices that underpin the existing model of school effectiveness.

Standards, Choice and Diversity in Education Discourse

The White Paper, *Choice and Diversity: A New Framework for Schools* (1992) published during the period of Conservative Government, identified five 'great themes':

- quality;
- diversity;
- increasing parental choice;
- greater autonomy for schools; and
- greater accountability as underscoring principles of educational change and development.

As can be seen below, these themes were to provide the framework in which the issue of educational standards was to be addressed subsequently in education.

Supported by the OECD (1989b) report *Schools and Quality: An International Report*, concerns about quality have remained an enduring theme in educational discourse and now incorporate also organization, systems and processes. In 1991 the Further Education Unit (FEU) published what was to become a highly influential document in the framing of the school effectiveness debate in England and Wales. *Quality Matters* (FEU, 1991: 2) positioned the concept of quality in education within the framework of manufacturing industry's definition of 'fitness for purpose' which, it argued, is 'arrived at through conformance to specification'. The FEU highlighted distinctions between the concepts of 'quality control', 'quality assurance', 'quality systems' and 'continuous quality improvement'. As is evident in our earlier discussion of Japanese and US work practices, the latter forms an integral part of the process of Total Quality Management (TQM) which places emphasis on 'the search for opportunities for improvement rather than maintaining current performance' (FEU, 1991: 2). The concepts of TQM which derived from the industrial model made famous by Deming and Juran during the 1950s and 1960s in the USA, and TQC central also to the Japanese production model, now feature centrally in the school effectiveness discourse through the work of writers such as Sallis (1993); Murgatroyd and Morgan (1992) and Greenwood and Gaunt (1994).

In education TQM transferred to the adoption of adequate measures 'to improve the quality of teaching and learning, to increase participation, and to improve attainment' (FEU, 1991: 3). Central to the concept of TQM is the need to generate a climate of 'not being satisfied' with performance. Organizations are required constantly to evaluate, research, analyse and measure needs, results and effectiveness and feedback as part of the process of continuous improvement (FEU, 1991). Thus it can be seen as subscribing to the ideological principles of *kaizen* discussed above. Forming part of a problem-solving approach, overall emphasis is on satisfying customers' needs and expectations and derives from production management.

Increasingly involved in the management of quality, or quality assurance, in schools and FE is the concept of 'soft-systems methodology' (SSM) developed by Peter Checkland in the 1970s (Kowszun, 1992: 1). SSM focuses on 'soft' systems such as corporate organizational problems, manufacturing performance and service marketing, and involves seven stages:

1   The problem situation unstructured.
2   The problem situation expressed.
3   Root definitions of relevant systems.
4   Conceptual models.
5   Comparison of 4 with 2.
6   Definition of feasible desirable outcomes.
7   Action to solve the problem or improve the situation (Kowszun, 1992: 3).

Again, this model incorporates key aspects of functional problem-solving and organizational learning grounded in the principles of continuous improvement central to *kaizen*. The concepts of TQM, *kaisha* and *kaizen* applied to education, will be discussed further in relation to school improvement in Chapter 5.

Diversity constitutes a principal variable in the consumer-driven market place where it serves to cater for ever-changing market/consumer demands. Within the educational policy framework it has related largely to the restructuring of the state education system by creating a diversified educational market allowing for increased consumer choice. Greater parental choice was provided in the 1988 ERA and featured in parental ballots in schools opting for GM status, and in open enrolment. Diversity in the range of educational provision was augmented by the Assisted Places Scheme (APS), Grant Maintained Schools (GMS), City Technology Colleges (CTCs). Announcing the introduction of CTCs in 1986, Kenneth Baker, then Secretary of State for Education, stated that 'education must be led by the users' and that this would be made possible by creating 'new free alternatives outside the maintained system' (quoted in Edwards et al., 1992: 153). In practice, this notion of diversity of choice essentially underscored the implementation of a highly selective semi-privatized educational system.

Its implementation was fraught with confusion and contradictions as was illustrated in the studies by Edwards et al. (1992). In their research of CTCs, they stated that:

the whole initiative was launched amid some confusion about whether CTCs were to be primarily a training ground for technological elite, for the technicians of a modern industrial society; or more generally for pupils and parents wanting 'a good education' with vocational relevance. (Edwards et al., 1992: 98)

These writers argued that in terms of offering a new choice to parents, CTCs served to create competition by 'creating alternatives to urban comprehensives' posing the threat of decreasing pupil numbers in the latter if standards did not improve. They maintained that 'being mostly situated in areas where secondary rolls are falling rapidly, CTCs can be seen as reinforcing that reliance on parental choice as a mechanism for closing "ineffective" schools' (Edwards et al., 1992: 155). Problems associated with diversity and choice in the Assisted Places Scheme are discussed in Chapter 8.

Local Autonomy

Local Management of Schools (LMS), central to the 1988 ERA, provided a pivotal element in the Conservative Government's project to de-bureaucratize local government. LMS was to allow for greater autonomy in decision making at school level. In effect, it provided the organizational and ideological basis for the emergence of management systems in state schooling and, sub-sequently, was to become also a central variable in the school effectiveness thesis. It was argued that:

Allowing schools to make decisions appropriate to their needs and to build on their strengths produces better and more committed centres of learning. By allowing resources to follow the pupil, we ensure that good schools can flourish. (DES, 1989e: 3)

Quite how effectively it has allowed schools to follow the pupil in terms of the diverse needs that exist in schools, and the unforeseen events and changing circumstances that serve to disrupt the normal patterns of school life is not quite clear. This has implications for considerations of equity especially in terms of how effectively schools can in practice respond to, for example, the needs of sporadic new intakes having different sets of needs to the existing school population.

Research by Gerwitz et al. (1995: 124) has shown some of the broader impacts of LMS, particularly, the pressure on pupil recruitment. They argue that:

Responding to the market is for many schools now a question of survival. A school with subscription levels too far below its standard number is in danger of being unviable and/or of having to make large scale redundancies. Most of our case-study schools have already used redundancies or 'natural wastage' to 'down size'. There is a persistent fear in low-recruiting schools of being caught within an irreversible cycle of decline.

Schools have been set in competition against one another, forcing them to change their ethos by cultivating specific marketable images, promotional events and presentation formats to capture parents in order to meet the needs of the market (Gerwitz et al., 1995). This gives some indication of the inequalities rationalized by the market. As is argued by Ranson and Stewart (1994: 49):

> under the guise of neutrality the market actively confirms and reinforces the preexisting social order of wealth and privilege . . . markets produce survivals and extinctions in a Darwinian zero-sum game. Markets, therefore, are political, that is, a way of making decisions about power in society, and they ensure that the already powerful win decisively.

The concepts of greater school autonomy and market accountability also underscored the constitution of school governing bodies. Schools were now to become more accountable to parents, employers and the community. The constitution of governing bodies had already been circumscribed in the 1986 Education Act which allowed the appointment of parents onto governing bodies. Schools were also to be allocated larger budgets depending on the size of their intake. Thus schools were to become more customer or consumer driven. As will be discussed below, customer needs subsequently became the *raison d'être* also of the internal systems of quality control put in place in schools.

Centralized Regulation – the Role of OFSTED

The 1992 White Paper *Choice and Diversity: A new framework for schools* that underscored Conservative educational policy, also provided for greater external regulatory controls. Standards were to be examined in 'regular and rigorous inspection under the watchful eye of the new and powerful Chief Inspector of Schools' (DES, 1992: 3). OFSTED findings are made available in nationally disseminated published reports. Although presented as the dissemination of information to consumers, the publication of inspection findings has served to reinforce the bi-polarization of school achievement in the identification of 'good' and 'bad' schools; 'successful' and 'failing' schools according to a standardized set of national criteria. This is the case despite the inherent heterogeneity of schools in terms of organizational culture, the broader cultural community, pupil in-take and socio-economic variables that impact on particular schools. Politically, the 'name and shame' policy that has accompanied OFSTED inspections has served to consolidate the demonization of teachers and the 'black listing' of schools. Teachers are thus forced to accept blame for their under-performing schools, and humiliated nationally. Schools in turn are then to be 'turned around', and re-invented as new production units. Thus school inspection has become a weapon with which to discipline and punish 'deviant' schools despite the different levels of need in disparate geographic and/or socio-economic regions in the country. OFSTED inspections therefore can be seen as serving to consolidate an ideological commitment to the 'zero-defect' guarantee that features in TQC practices operating in industry.

The overall emphasis on teacher accountability since 1988 has been reinforced in the policy framework of New Labour. Claiming 'excellence for everyone' as their guiding motif, the New Labour Government is committed to 'zero-tolerance of underperformance' in the education service including schools, teachers and LEAs (DfEE, 1997: 12). Combined with the rigidities inherent in the National Curriculum framework, including its assessment processes and the internal and external controls exercised over the entire schooling process, OFSTED inspections on a nation-wide basis serve to consolidate the totalizing 'gaze' of TQM within education as a whole. Whilst its educational emphasis is on monitoring the effectiveness of schools in relation to their catering for the needs of pupils and the expectations of parents, ideologically, it constitutes a powerful means of policing school and education process. With its social control function typified by strong sur-veillance exercised over the performativity of the whole schooling process, the procedure of OFSTED inspections can be seen as sharing commonalities with the concept of 'neo-Fordism/neo-Taylorism' discussed above. Ultimately, the OFSTED inspection process can be seen as serving to consolidate a technocratic power base.

The language of policing features centrally in the New Labour framework in which the notion of 'zero tolerance of underperformance' is supported by a 'Standards Task Force' under the chair of the Secretary of State, with the Chief Inspector of Schools and the Director of Education for Birmingham as vice chairs, and the 'Standards and Effectiveness Unit' (SEU) (DfEE, 1997). The eclectic borrowing of concepts and categories from a wide range of frameworks is particularly evident in the White Paper, *Excellence in Schools* (DfEE, 1997). Launched as 'crusaders' of the standards and quality cause, SEU has the remit to 'challenge LEAs and schools about their endeavours to raise standards, learn from their experience, question their assumptions, and inform them about examples of best practice' (DfEE, 1997: 32). The sharing of 'best practice' is to be consolidated in a national database that can be accessed by all schools. This strategy, combined with the work of the SEU and the setting up of Education Action Zones, share similarities with the continuous improvement principles of *kaizen* and TQM discussed above. The difference is that here it takes place not only within the micro-context of individual school process but also under the omnipotent and omniscient gaze of centralized, national technologies of control.

It is somewhat ironic that the deregulated market introduced into the educational system through the 1988 ERA, typified by increased parental choice, LMS, opting out and GM schools exists in contradiction with the strong forms of control that inhere in the 'gaze' that penetrates the whole educational process. This structural rigidity leaves little opportunity for real innovation and autonomy in schools. Another ironic outcome is that within an ideological framework centred on de-bureaucratization and the dispersal of power controls embodied in flexible work processes, new forms and layers of bureaucracy have emerged within the school organization itself, and the overall education system.

Qua Flexibility?

How successfully then are schools approximating the 'flexible firm' able to respond to rapid and evolving need as is described in the post-Fordist framework? If, as is argued by Avis (1996: 75), 'post-Fordist firms thrive on chaos', then the model of schooling underscored by the National Curriculum and monitoring and assessment framework of the 1988 ERA, and reinforced by the New Labour drive for total quality management, precludes itself from being called 'post-Fordist'. The post-ERA education system is constituted in rigid frameworks and hierarchies of strong supervisory control. As such, it seemingly shares more commonalities with the totalizing 'gaze' and labour intensive principles that inhere in 'neo-Fordist' or 'neo-Taylorist' work practices and worker awarenesses, than with the liberating qualities of craft labour described in the 'post-Fordist' proposition. And thus it replicates workers' experiences in manufacturing industry (Tomaney, 1990; Pollert, 1988; Wolf, 1984).

Key issues for debate revolve around:

- systematized forms of surveillance that constitute an integral part of the culture of the organization; and
- the emphasis on flexible work practices grounded in a process of ongoing task-oriented learning within a rigidly defined and monitored framework.

More important is the overall emphasis on not only total quality control, but also the intensification of the work process and the totalizing gaze of self-monitoring in the educational production process. The paradox is that time spent on quality assurance mechanisms can be distracting from the qualitative aspects of the job itself, such as learning processes and the affective and aesthetic aspects of teaching and learning. There are more contradictions. Implicit in the monitoring gaze of OFSTED is the scope that it has to weed out 'bad' teachers, and thus to purge the 'bugs' in the system. But at the same time, 'zero-tolerance' of defects, whilst theoretically supporting the effectiveness drive, also has the potential to create job insecurity amongst teachers. The climate of fear and uncertainty generated by OFSTED inspections and re-inspections are major stress factors operating in many schools. Of increasing concern is the extent to which it relies on the accumulation of highly subjective information.

Undoubtedly, individual schools can and do organize themselves in flexible work teams able to respond to different types and levels of need that may arise within the context of everyday life in schools. Nevertheless, they do so within clearly demarcated national assessment criteria. How schools choose to operate, and where they would place emphasis, would also depend to a large extent on their collective interpretation of 'quality', the vision of the head teacher and the particular management style adopted. Ball (1997) has shown in his study of practice in Martineau, that the head teacher's charisma plays an important part of the relative success of particular schools in fulfilling their corporate aims.

Post-Fordist Schools?

Evidently then, many work practices that have evolved in schools approximate both the Japanese and US TQM model of production and worker management. Thus we have teaching staff organized into teams working according to the principles that frame the concepts of 'quality circles' and 'cellular technologies' adapted to education. At a deeper level, however, the incorporation of TQM approaches into management systems of schools ultimately shape the culture of teaching, learning and management throughout the whole organization. And, as we stated earlier, these are now subjected to systematized policing of 'zero-tolerance of defects' by special centrally appointed national 'Task Forces' and OFSTED.

Teachers have, in line with the Japanese concept of *kaisha* or 'companyism', to pledge their loyalty to the school and its development plan (SDP). However, unlike their Japanese industrial counterparts they do not have the same or equivalent benefits such as the security of lifetime employment or, necessarily, seniority-based promotion. Within the free market that operates in education the Darwinian principle of 'survival of the fittest' underscores staff selection. That is to say, those who can adapt and change to accommodate evolving conditions have a better chance of surviving. Ironically, again, this does not necessarily imply the retention of good educators. For teachers are more than mere functionaries within the work process, and educational achievement is more than achieving standardized targets. Teachers play a key role in the shaping of not only functional and cognitive skills and knowledges but also the affective, social and aesthetic development of the child as a whole person. Moreover, in addressing issues of equity in and through their teaching, and providing pupils with the skills, knowledge and critical awarenesses needed to interpret and understand their social world, teachers are fundamentally cultural workers.

Within the present milieu, as is the case with their industrial counterparts, teachers are required to be multiskilled, flexible and able to adjust to evolving needs. Flexible job demarcation means that they can be shifted from one set of responsibilities to another as an integral part of their job experience.

Thus, we find at middle management level, Heads of Year (HOYs) who may also, simultaneously, be doing the job of Head of Department (HOD); or the HOD whilst also being a group tutor and subject-teacher; or in the Primary Phase, being a Deputy Head Teacher with overall responsibility for staff development and time table, whilst at the same time also having to fulfil their role as a class or subject teacher in addition to having management responsibilities as subject specialist. These multi-levelled responsibilities bring with them different kinds and degrees of stress, and are not necessarily all remunerated. Although multiskilling and flexibility to adjust to changing demands may provide for a cost-effective education service, it does so without consideration for its human cost.

The education system as a whole, now more than ever, represents a site of production organized around centrally defined principles of quality, choice and accountability to the customer as well as to bureaucratic powers of surveillance. Schools feature as individual production units existing in competition with other schools, which are not necessarily of equivalent status. Again, this shows the inequality inherent in the processes of the market.

Many of the new innovative organizational and entrepreneural approaches that have emerged in schools during the past decade operate alongside older forms of management and control (Ball, 1997). Thus we have the rigidity of Fordism sitting alongside new market-sensitive flexible forms of work organization represented in the neo-liberal framework. As we could see in Chapter 2, hybridity in organizational and management approaches is not specific to this educational milieu. It also prevailed during the 1970s when many schools, whilst they adhered ideologically to the principles of comprehensive education, nevertheless, still chose to stream, band and place pupils with special educational needs in withdrawal classes. Thus whilst, *ideologically*, the structural changes would seem to indicate definitive changes which herald a 'new historic bloc' (Bonefeld, 1987) in the organization of education, in *systemic* terms there are strong continuities with past forms of educational control.

Summary

In this chapter we have highlighted the fact that education constitutes an integral part of society and culture and, therefore, has to be seen as being relational. That is to say, the nature of the changes taking place in school organization can be understood properly only if they are examined in relation to the external events that have given legitimacy to particular practices and processes – and, by that fact, the exclusion of different possibilities. Instead of selecting out systems, process and 'performativity' as *the* key organizing principles – which is the case in the prevailing school effectiveness framework, analysis needs to acknowledge discursivity. This includes acknowledgement of the fact that:

- education is grounded in particular forms of social relations that are circumscribed and sustained by complex societal power networks, practices and processes. And, at the same time, account needs to be taken of the inherently disordered and unstable nature of determining forces, and the different value interests that underpin the prevailing model of educational change. The past decade has been a period of relentless change in education;
- the quality control processes put into place to sustain the dominant model of educational change and development have discursive impacts and effects. This necessarily includes variables such as equity, social justice and values as these relate to the lives of those involved in education (teachers and pupils) as well as the communities in which they live and work;
- education operates within an organically interactive context traversed by a diverse range of often conflicting and contradictory individual, cultural and institutional meanings. As is argued by Angus (1993: 342):

> the embeddedness of schooling within wider social dynamics and power relationships means that context is relational, dynamic and interactive such that, for instance, schools and schooling are influenced by, but also influence, the cultural milieu of the society in which they are embedded. They articulate with other sectors of the social formation and contribute to power relations and widely shared beliefs across sectors of society and macro-cultures.

The issues raised throughout this chapter have highlighted the fact that the relative 'effectiveness' (or not) of schools needs to be seen and understood in relation to the influences of a variety of social, political and cultural factors. Thus educational discussions need to incorporate wider sets of questions that transcend circumscribed taxonomies of school effectiveness within the narrow confines of bureaucratic power processes. They need to address issues related to the motivations of the policy drivers; the primary significations that give meaning to the particular notion of social change that predominates; cultural power and the role of education within a reconceptualized transformative democratic polity. Educational change and development are intrinsically political.

Questions
1 What do you understand by:
(a)   Fordism and Post-Fordism
(b)   the capital accumulation process
(c)   the flexible firm
(d)   *kaizen*

(e)   the learning society

(f)   total quality management

2   Which aspects of schooling are screened out by the application of TQM practices in schools?

3   In terms of the multiskilling implied in flexible work practices in schools, how do teachers balance their managerial duties with their multiple responsibilities as teachers? What are the impacts of this on pupils' learning?

4   To what extent does your school approximate the notion of the 'flexible firm'?

Chapter 4

Managing School Effectiveness: New Managerialism, Change and the Reconfiguration of Power

School effectiveness is a microtechnology of change. Change is brought about by a focus on the school as a site-based system to be managed. In this chapter, we wish to argue that the school effectiveness movement is an example of new managerialism in education. Education, like other public services, is now characterized by a range of structural realignments, new relationships between purchasers and providers and new coalitions between management and politics. Neo-liberalism has informed the development of social policy and policy has been implemented via the structures and value system of new managerialism. New managerialism in education has implied that the 3 Rs are best achieved via the 3 Es (economy, efficiency and effectiveness). Institutional analysis has replaced sociology of education (Ryan, 1995). Drawing on principles of systems theory advocated in the 1980s by influential reports such as the Hargreaves Report (1984), school effectiveness is an output-oriented, plan-based ideology. The school is seen as a series of inter-related elements which transform various inputs into desired outputs. As we argued in Chapter 3, it involves new structures, new rationalities and new regimes of regulation, introduced largely from the corporate context of the private sector ostensibly to promote efficiency, productivity, quality and cost-effectiveness in the public services. Values, as well as technologies and drive systems from the cultural world of business and commerce have been imported into education, bringing with them new meanings, priorities and truths.

As we have already argued, school effectiveness is discursively intertextual, informed by an eclectic set of concepts. As part of education reform in Britain, school effectiveness draws upon a range of theoretical approaches, including management and organization studies, to legitimate itself as a self-evidently correct framework for change. It is part of the growing apparatus of performance evaluation. Ideas about educational change have been reworked and re-articulated in a new configuration of power. The reforms, revolutions and realignments of the 1980s produced new norms and discourses for managing the economic crisis. There was a perceived need to try and get more for less out of the public services. However, as Hoggett (1996: 14) indicates, the cash limited nature of public service funding forces the players to engage in a zero-sum game in which the 'market is only expandable at the expense of another'. Hence the market propels organizations into individualistic, competitive activity (Ball, 1993). With the introduction of Local Management of Schools (LMS), schools have become 'semi-autonomous operating units' (Levacic, 1993: 181). Within these units, policy networks of schools, managers, the state, governors and parents have been formed to operationalize the changes.

Implementation of macro value systems to the microprocesses of the organization have been mediated through new managerialism. Wider political aims linked to the economics of education have been distilled into taxonomies, checklists and recipes for effectiveness. Changes have been materially and discursively driven, with school effectiveness and improvement becoming dominant discourses of educational change. The hegemonic function of discourses was discussed by Clarke and Newman (1997: 39/40):

> Discourses seek to mobilise – to build alliances and support for specific social projects. They aim to establish themselves as normalised 'truths', the self-evidently correct frameworks of thought and action.

The 1980s witnessed an intersection of political rationalities with management technologies. A new interface between management and professionalism emerged. The 'truth' of new managerialism as a transformative device was spoken by key politicians, such as Michael Heseltine, the Secretary of State for the Environment in 1980:

> Efficient management is the key to the [national] revival . . . And the management ethos must run right through our national life – private and public companies, civil service, nationalised industries, local government, the National Health Service. (Heseltine, quoted in Pollitt, 1993: 3)

Underpinning this statement was the requirement for the public services to earn their legitimacy and to demonstrate performance (Morley, 1997a).

School effectiveness combines culture management (the creation of purposes and meanings) with performance management (measuring what really matters). Performance is now an organizational responsibility. Generally, in the public services, the performance ethos has created an 'audit explosion', with a proliferation of evaluative procedures (Power, 1994; Strathern, 1997). Audit is a modernist construction, based on a conflation of measures with targets. There is a modernist, rationalist belief that the complexities of the social world can be measured and recorded with the appropriate instruments and technologies. Specific performance indicators are selected to illustrate effectiveness and individuals and organizations are graded in relation to these signifiers. The results then provide a reified reading of reality, which becomes a truth.

Schools, like other public service institutions over the last two decades, have been subject to 'human accounting'. The introduction of markets and managers has been a generic transformational device designed to restructure and reorient public service provision. The common elements have involved site-based management, the language of improvement and budgetary devolution. Funding regimes have become structuring mechanisms. Decision making, priorities, service provision are determined by financial considerations. There are also financial consequences to quality audits, with resources allocated and withdrawn according to performance. Schools have been reinvented as financial bodies, and an audit culture has emerged. Power (1994: 36–37) notes:

> What is audited is whether there is a system which embodies standards and the standards of performance themselves are shaped by the need to be auditable . . . audit becomes a formal 'loop' by which the system observes itself.

In this analysis, school effectiveness is a structure which allows schools to model their ability to perform adequately, or not. Schools are measured according to pre-set standardized criteria of what an effective school would look like. Ball (1997: 318) argues that the idea of a 'good' school has been reduced to 'a set of simple perfomativities and representations'. The auditing gaze is both internal and external, as schools are subjected to inspection on a four/five and now six-year cycle. There is also a strong element of self-scrutiny. This self-regulation is an example of how power can be capillary, rather than monolithic. A capillary notion of power suggests that power operates everywhere in everyday transactions. It is totalizing in so far as it is rehearsed in inter and intrapersonal relations, as well as in structures (Morley, 1998a).

New managerialism represents the atomization of control. Responsibility is dispersed and devolved so that every organizational member is burdened with income generation, quality, standards and performance. In the elision of teacher with manager, emphasis has shifted from job specification to performance specification. There is also a powerful mechanism of disciplining and self-disciplining. As Thrupp (1998) argues, regulatory organizations such as OFSTED gain their ideological power from holding school staff responsible for school effectiveness. This strategy has its consequences. A central paradox of new managerialism in education is the way in which output has been ostensibly enhanced at the same time as stress, low morale, low recruitment and early retirement among educators have increased. The discourse of regulation and blame is driving teachers out of the profession *en masse*, and creating a crisis in recruitment (Brimblecombe et al., 1996; Cooper and Kelly, 1993; Jeffrey and Woods, 1996; Travers and Cooper, 1996). There is a myth that increasing the workload for teachers results in enhanced effectiveness (Reay, 1998). While there appears to be a consensualist assumption regarding mission, targets, and commitment to quality and customer responsiveness, educators are faced with increasing class sizes, longer working hours, and disappearing job security. A key question is who benefits from this construction of effectiveness and what are the costs?

Regulating the Chaos

New managerialism relates to both macro economic policy and neo-Fordist or neo-Taylorist work regimes. A fundamental belief is that objectives of social policy can be promoted at a lower cost when the appropriate management techniques are applied to the public services. The indeterminacy of the social world can be regulated and controlled by effective management. Ball (1990) notes that the term 'management' is the linguistic antithesis to chaos, and implies rationality in the face of unruliness. There are strong moral undertones masked as a neutral technology. New managerialism bases its status on early Taylorist claims that management is a scientific discipline. Hence, a technicist industry has developed, based on a rationalist epistemology of change. Pollitt (1993: 15) observes:

> Then, as now, it was supposed that, if only management and administration could be established as a scientific discipline, then public officials would be better protected against the irrationality of 'political interference'.

Maidment and Thompson (1993: 25) remind us that:

> The Conservative government that was elected in 1979 wished to 'roll back the frontiers of the state'. It wished to do so by altering the balance between modes of coordination within British society as a whole, between market and non-market; it wished to alter the way in which Britain was managed.

The result has been the development of competing moral systems with welfare principles in opposition to market principles or 'guardian versus commercial' syndromes (Jacobs, 1992).

School effectiveness has created new institutional norms and patterns, and new logics of appropriateness. New organizational forms are thought to hold the key to means–ends efficiency and quality assurance in education. Clarke and Newman (1997: ix) describe managerialism:

> as a cultural formation and a distinctive set of ideologies and practices which form one of the underpinnings of an emergent political settlement.

Central to new managerialism is the promotion of a corporate mission, with goals, targets, monitoring procedures and performance measurement. Responsibility is devolved and increased responsiveness to clients/customers is alleged. The creation of quasi markets and structural decentralization have created a new power base from which managers can operate. This has taken place at a time when the powers of central government have been substantially increased in education. However, in new managerialism, power is also ostensibly located with clients, the community and competing organizations. There are cascading, or top down, levels of power. There is an appearance of relative autonomy, but this is carefully screened by the gaze of authoritarian central controls. Clarke, Cochrane and McLaughlin (1994) believe that these developments are part of a wider ideological process which has transformed relations of power, culture, control and accountability, and this is linked to social policy changes which reflect an ongoing reconceptualization and restructuring of the state.

School effectiveness depicts a transition from a monopolistic to a competitive mode of production in education. Rather than a flexible system suggested by the notion of the 'free market', schools and other public service organizations are to be run like rationally structured machines. In the context of the crisis of Fordist hegemony, falling or low educational standards represented a structural crisis – that is the difference between theory and reality. Overcoming what was perceived as a major crisis of standards and academic attainment in education seemed to depend on strategies and struggles concerning organizational forms. Underpinning this move was the desire to standardize and reduce product variety in education. Quality can only be evaluated when like is compared with like. School effectiveness as part of the change agenda has attempted to reduce heterogeneity in organizational forms. Instead of recognizing diversity and pluralism, there is an assumption that there is one best way of doing things and that this will work for all organizations, communities and individuals. This has resulted in an industrialization of education. Clarke and Newman (1997: 80) observe that there are now 'demands for organisations to possess systems that will generate comparable information to facilitate the process of evaluation'. Clarke and Newman (1997) describe the tendency of organizations to adopt similar forms as 'isomorphism'. This implies that change is homogeneous and unilinear and ignores differences in quality and kind. We explore this concept further in relation to school improvement in Chapter 5.

These new logics and forms of knowledge have been given legitimizing frameworks. The school effectiveness movement has attempted to produce a common value system and common representations of reality such as taxonomies, checklists, performance indicators, league tables and target-setting exercises. Taxonomies define the exact configuration of organizational forms and represent a set of bounded rationalities. They are a vision of purity, with a connection between signs and meanings. However, there are questions about the location of the unrepresentable, such as the affective domain and the hidden curriculum. For example, Shaw (1990: 273) argues that the hidden curriculum is about:

> values, conducts, political positions, ways of perceiving and understanding reality, the self and others, and important commitments of a social and moral kind are transmitted in a largely uncontrolled and to some extent unplanned way, without the teachers or the pupils being aware in a conscious analytical way of what is happening.

Effectiveness is a term with multiple meanings, but these have been reduced and sanitized to exclude the areas mentioned in the above quotation. Concepts of change embodied in school effectiveness have excluded other views of what could or should be changed, measured or monitored. School effectiveness taxonomies are hierarchies of interests, involving value judgements about the relative importance of different organizational goals. The certainty could be said to lack humility or reflexivity. For example, the position of the observer, or compiler of the taxonomies of effectiveness is not subjected to the same critical analysis as that of the organization under scrutiny. The role of values is skirted and there is an emphasis on what works rather than whose interests are being served. However, the values of the market now predominate. As Shaw (1990: 274) argues there has been a 'greater specification and stipulation of the teaching task, in content, method and approach'. Schools are now constructed as product-oriented organizations, subject to market forces, and whose primary purpose is contribution to wealth creation. (Shaw, 1990)

Parker (1997: 152) views the outcomes' imperative, with relentless checklists and taxonomies, as crude measures of quality:

> We don't take a checklist to the theatre to discover whether the play was good or to find out whether or not we really enjoyed it. And neither should we take one to the school, the classroom or the students.

This would seem to suggest that standardization is in opposition to creativity and aesthetics. In a system of rule-following and pattern-recognizing order replaces interpretative freedom (Bauman, 1997). However, for many, interpretative freedom in education was causally linked to low standards, and there needed to be an insertion of certainties and benchmarks. Taxonomies, with their conceptual boundaries, prescribe and limit how one perceives and experiences one's institution. The environment is presented and pre-interpreted by a series of common-sense constructs. School effectiveness has represented a shift from abstraction to empiricism, from reflection to action. The New Right discursively positioned the old regime as a type of imprecise quagmire, populated by unruly teachers, an unregulated curriculum and falling standards (see Figure 4.1). The chaos had to be purified and distilled into lean, minimalist blueprints for success.

School effectiveness, like most dogmas, presents its own version of damnation – the failing school. Bauman (1997: 11) suggests that 'each order has its own disorders; each model of purity has its own dirt that needs to be swept away'. Levi-Strauss (cited in Bauman, 1997: 18) explores anthropologically, systems for making the different similar. One way was *anthropophagic* – annihilating the strangers by devouring them and then metabolically transforming them into a tissue indistinguishable from one's own. The other strategy was *anthropoemic*: vomiting – banishing, confining and expelling the strangers. When all else failed, the strangers were physically destroyed. In the framework of effectiveness, schools that cannot be transformed are closed down (Tomlinson, 1998). The system purges itself of impurities.

Figure 4.1:   School effectiveness as an example of the New Right ideological project

- The public services required to demonstrate legitimacy;
- Introduction of new regimes of truth e.g. quality, accountability;
- Emphasis on the microprocesses of the organization;
- Management as the transformative device;
- New Managerialism – An intersection of political rationalities with management technologies;
- Means – ends arguments. Output-oriented, plan-based ideology;
- Values, as well as technologies imported from business world;
- The role and function of values is skirted and there is an emphasis on what works rather than whose interests are being served;
- Growing apparatus of performance evaluation;
- Performance is now an organizational responsibility;
- Emphasis on measurement and quantification;
- Exclusion of the affective domain and the marginalization of non-assessed fields of inquiry;
- Deprofessionalization/demonization/regulation of teachers. Making education teacher-proof;
- The Audit Explosion and Human Accounting – regulation, surveillance, inspections, 'steering at a distance', internal and external gaze;
- Competition thought to stimulate raising of standards;
- Funding regimes have become structuring mechanisms;
- Standardization and reduction of product variety in education. Attempts to establish a common value system;
- Heroic formulation of leaders. Unproblematic construction of hierarchical basis of leadership;
- The reconstructed headteacher/manager as a systems engineer;
- Dispersed management responsibility. All organizational members responsible for income generation/standards/productivity;
- Cognitive restructuring of professionals. Docile bodies. Compliance culture;
- The child reduced to a cognitive, rather than a social entity;
- Parentocracy, consumerism, entitlements and Darwinian selection i.e. the survival of the fittest schools;
- Schools evolve elaborate procedures to protect standards i.e. 'Cream-skimming and boundary setting' (Clarke and Newman, 1997);
- Reconstruction of purchasers/consumers without acknowledgement of social power, barriers to participation and inequalities;
- Equity is off the agenda. Reinvention of the universal subject. Teachers and learners are deracialized, declassed, degendered and disembodied;
- The rise of communitarianism. New forms of governance. Perceived as democratization and/or surveillance;
- New partnerships and policy networks – school governors, links with industry;
- A rationalist epistemology of change i.e. a theory of change that is linear, algorythmic and consensual with an input/output emphasis.

A central paradox in school effectiveness work is the extent to which management and effectiveness are presented as neutral concepts, while forming a major part of the New Right educational reform agenda (see Figure 4.1). The market has been flooded with 'how to' literature, particularly in relation to education management (e.g. Caldwell and Spinks, 1988; 1992). Education has been reduced to site management problematics that are amenable to management solutions. Angus (1994: 81) indicates that educators are:

> . . . encouraged not to question the social and political conditions of their work but to get on and do the job by focussing on their own little domain of the school.

Deem, Brehony and Heath (1995: 27) also note how school governors, as 'guardians of efficiency and effectiveness' are only concerned with the good of the particular school they govern. There has been a process of domestication and boundary setting, with schools turning inwards to focus on microper-formance, creating new forms of tribalism and territoriality.

This shift from macropolitical factors to the microsphere of the school has been one of the most controversial aspects of school effectiveness. The language used in education reform and school effectiveness appropriates certain understandings of sociological concepts such as democracy, empower-ment, participation, choice, and community (Angus, 1994; Morley, 1995). This is juxtaposed with the logic of the market and language and concepts from management studies such as accountability, quality, and efficiency. With new managerialism, a particular form of citizenship is being reinforced, one that is not socially differentiated. As Clarke and Newman (1997: xiii) indicate new managerialist terms such as 'stakeholders', 'customers', 'citizens' mask important forms of differentiation around 'race', gender, sexualities, class and other social formations.

The Heroic Formulation of Leadership

New managerialism has glamourized the manager. As Clarke and Newman (1997: 36) humorously point out, the new image has transformed 'the bureaucratic time-server to dynamic leader'. The discursively reconstituted functionary is now a charismatic change agent and risk-taker, associated with innovation, corporate culture and enterprise. The enterprise culture has allowed public service managers the opportunity to demonstrate their con-nection to the business world, with pressures and incentives operating at a number of levels. There has been a cognitive restructuring of public service workers, particularly the professionals who are now required to operate managerially. In the juxtaposition of professionalism with managerialism, there has been a bureaucratization of professionalism and a new compliance culture. As Clarke and Newman (1997) mention there has been the creation of new subjects who enact the discourse of new managerialism. This is evocative of the concept of *kaisha* that we described in Chapter 3. Corporate loyalty and organizational performance are cornerstones of new managerialism and school effectiveness, both in terms of advertising results, but also in the way that rituals are enacted regardless of their efficacy. So, schools produce action plans, mission statements, targets, strategies and visions as a matter of symbolic compliance or legitimation – that is, producing the symbols that schools are expected to have.

The reconstructed headteacher is a systems engineer. School effectiveness requires complex investment decisions. Just as there have been typologies of the effective school, so too is there a set of assumptions about what constitutes effective leadership. Leadership is a controversial concept, often embedded within classic hierarchical thinking and polarized notions of the leaders and the led. However, in school effectiveness it is represented as automatically benign and upbeat. Leaders are represented as uncontested figures 'who purport to restrict themselves to the realms of fact, means and measurable effectiveness (Wilcox, 1997: 252). The unproblematic construction of leadership and shared vision in school effectiveness research implies that organizational culture is based on consensus, rather than conflict (Ball, 1987; Morley, 1999). It ignores the micropolitical processes in the school and the way in which power relations and competing interests interact with change programmes. Clegg (1990: 19) explains how:

> Organisation, conceived in terms of its modernist antecedents, implies a degree of legal and more normative unity, a single centre of calculation and classification, a relatively unambiguous distribution of power and influence, and a setting for action sufficiently uniform for *similar actions* to be expected to bring *similar consequences* for the whole and thus to be interpreted in a similar way.

A central contradiction in school effectiveness is that the school, as an organization, is presented both as a unified structure and a series of fractured categories. It is represented as both stable and fluidly amenable to deconstruction and change. Organizational culture is seen as a substance to be shaped and manipulated in the interests of school effectiveness. Reay (1998) highlights a further contradiction in so far as school effectiveness discourses give primacy to leadership skills and the role of the head teacher, while simultaneously purporting to value team-building and collegiality. New managerialism has reinforced the concept of corporatism. Again, like the concept of *kaisha* described in Chapter 3, this requires loyalty and compliance, with heavy penalties for dissent. There is the belief that meanings, values and beliefs are shared, and that these are disconnected from issues of power, control and hierarchy. Concepts such as participation are perceived as harmonious, bonding processes, rather than the differentiated representation of interest groups. Equally, barriers to participation, such as gender, 'race', social class, sexual orientation and disability are left unexplored. It is assumed that the leader will intuitively understand what is in the best interests of the school, and will be able to represent the interests of others. The leader is thought to embody the most appropriate values and visions for everyone concerned. Complex educational issues are reduced to challenges for different management techniques and strategies. Angus (1994: 85) notes how:

> . . . it is believed that leaders of vision are able to bring about a negotiated order which accords with their own definitions and purposes and ensures that any change is directed into reasonable, predictable channels by their own overriding moral force. Other organisational participants, such as teachers, parents and students . . . are generally viewed as passive recipients of the leader's vision.

Headteachers are now viewed in much the same light as chief executives in industry.

Consumerism, Parentocracy and Empowerment

A key concept in reform of the public services has been empowerment (Morley, 1995, 1998b). In education, empowerment is now embedded in the discourse of parental rights and choice. This has been part of the reasoning for the introduction of league tables and other signifiers of productivity. An essential feature of marketization has been the move towards customer-centred services. This is thought to drive organizational dynamism and to dislodge the complacency of state monopolies and producer capture. It would be unhelpful to degenerate into another past/future binary by suggesting that all that was associated with the old regime was good, and that the new culture is uniformly bad. The situation is more complex. The discourse of choice and consumer power can be attractive to members of the community who have traditionally experienced powerlessness and frustration in relation to powerful organizations. Cox (1992: 23–24) states:

> There is a powerful resonance in assertions that contrast the benefits of being a consumer in a free market with the dependence and subordination implied by being a client, patient, tenant or pupil in a professionally domin-ated and often patronizing, sexist and racially biased public service.

However, Clarke and Newman (1997: 67) argue that while managerialism 'challenges the bureaucratic and often paternalistic basis of the normative power of bureau-professional regimes', it can also offer a 'different set of logics and constraints'. Clarke and Newman (1997) believe that public services have been forced into a system of 'cream-skimming and boundary setting' in order to maintain economic viability. In relation to schools, this can involve a degree of selection that will guarantee success in the league tables. In this respect, school effectiveness can be manipulated by more powerful players in the education market.

Consumerism constructs parents as active service users, defining needs and wants. However, it is based on public choice theory and it has been argued that parental choice is a form of popular capitalism, and indeed the rhetoric of choice is a disguised class strategy. Recent research into parental choice (Bowe, Ball, and Gerwitz, 1994; Reay, 1996) notes how parents' cultural capital and social class backgrounds were key determinants in the choice of schools. A central conclusion has been that the outcome of marketization has increased, rather than decreased social reproduction in education (Butterfield, 1998). In this framework of individualism, working-class parents are con-structed as bad consumers, a new form of impurity. Recent parental choice research is also evocative of Coleman's earlier findings about links between educational attainment and socio-economic backgrounds (Coleman, 1966).

Education represents both a public and a private good. Marketization has transformed it into a commodity, a product one consumes. All markets are social constructions. They constitute sites in which different players with different power compete for resources and services according to fluctuating rules (Hoggett, 1996). More privileged parents continue to have the social power to enable them to decode the educational system, identify appropriate questions and provide material resources for transport, tutoring and so on. Social and material circumstances of working class parents, alongside internalized oppression, mean that they are often forced to settle for the nearest school, regardless of what it has to offer. On a more positive note, this can also be perceived as a commitment to the local community and investment in one's neighbourhood. While we would challenge the homogenizing distortions embedded in some of the social class classifications, it would appear that only certain parents are empowered. The 1980 Education Act stipulated that the local education authority and school governors must comply with parental choice of school. However, the Hillgate Group (1986: 14) draw attention to some of the contradictions:

> On the same page we are told that parents should be free to send their children to any school of their choice, while, at the same time, 'schools should have the right to control their own admissions'

It would appear that it is often more a question of chosen parents than parental choice.

Parental choice is discursively constructed both as consumer empowerment and further surveillance of schools and teachers. Parents have been incorporated into the implementation of school effectiveness. Levacic (1993: 186) argues that the government has put in place two systems of accountability:

> One is hierarchical regulation in the form of the national curriculum, inspection to judge the quality of its delivery in schools and quantitative measures derived from national testing. The other mode of accountability is the market itself, relying on parental judgement to confirm through school choice which are good schools and which are poor schools.

League tables are a form of hierarchical regulation. The issue of the efficacy and influence of league tables as an index of quality have been the subject of substantial debate. The influential Hargreaves Report (1984) represented an early contribution to school effectiveness research. The advice at that time was that examination results were only part of parental rationale for choice.

> The ILEA rightly takes performance in 16 plus examinations as one measure of school effectiveness and, in so doing, reflects public and parental opinion . . . we have received substantial evidence from a wide variety of witnesses that too much emphasis is now placed on performance in public examinations as a criterion of school effectiveness. (Hargreaves, 1984: 10)

It would seem that, in spite of the government's preoccupation with league tables as indicators of quality, many parents of differing class backgrounds continue to make choices based on impressions, rumour, reputation, or related to the affective domain. Desire for their children's happiness and a sense of satisfaction with the school's ambience and ethos influence parents' choices. This indicates that, even in the context of new managerialism, choice is still chaotic and irrational and hence notoriously difficult to manage.

The Rise of Communitarianism

Whereas much of the thinking from sociology and consideration of social contexts have been eroded in school effectiveness, there has been a growing preoccupation with the concept of community. Increased community participation in the public services has been an aim of New Right reform (see Figure 4.1). Following the recommendations of the Taylor Committee (Taylor, 1977), the 1980 Education Act stipulated that elected parents and teachers must serve on the governing bodies of schools (Deem, Brehony and Heath, 1995). Links with the community are often included in taxonomies for effectiveness. However, the term 'community' is polysemic, with a multitude of meanings and interpretations. Community is seen as an alternative to state domination, that is, a type of people power. It is also a mechanism for softening the individual consumption involved in marketization. Community has provided a recurrent reference point across a range of public services e.g. community policing, care in the community, community relations councils, community service, community health councils, community nursing. The spectacularly unpopular poll tax, based on *individual* consumption of services, was euphemistically named a community charge.

Increased community participation in the public services has been an aim of New Right reform. Clarke and Newman (1997: 131) comment:

> The rediscovery of 'community' has also emerged in the context of the impoverishment of the public realm effected by New Right ideology and policy. Community addresses the sense of loss created by the claim that 'there is no such thing as society'.

The new civic discourse of obligatory partnerships is perceived as both empowering for consumers and as a political device for achieving change without governmental financial burden. The latter is also seen as a way of central government distancing itself from unpopular decisions such as school and hospital closures. This is another example of the 'steering at a distance' syndrome. 'Community' has also become a euphemism for reduction of state financial support e.g. care in the community.

Globalization means that the rise of communities is no longer restricted by place. In recent sociological literature, reference can be found to 'moral communities' (Weeks, 1991), 'transnational communities' (McGrew, 1992), 'virtual communities' (Rheingold, 1993). Like the term empowerment, community has lost its grassroots, radical edge and has been incorporated into government policy. One view is that it is seen to operate as a 'hooray' word. Raymond Williams (1976: 66) observed that the term 'community' 'seems never to be used unfavourably.' However, this construction is changing. Whereas it can be concerned with neighbourhood, shared values, identity, interests, activism, partnerships, social movements, support, more recently it has also become associated with accountability and regulation. Parry et al. (1987: 245) quote an Oldham councillor who said, 'when I hear the word "community" I reach for my gun'. In this context, community links were perceived as constraints, interference and regimes of regulation. In education, the term 'community' was often used to refer to particular social groups of parents, especially black parents. Now, it also incorporates partnerships with business and industry.

The concept of community can suggest a homogeneity of interests without addressing divisions and hierarchies along lines of gender, age, social class, sexual orientation, ethnicity, disabilities and other sociological variables. There is an issue of representation and leadership. Bauman (1995: 153) expresses the view that 'the self-gestation of a community requires shouting down the competitors and numbing the dissidents'. Equally, 'communities' can close ranks to keep those deemed as 'other' on the outside. The community is not always a friend to education. There have been several recent 'community' campaigns to block the introduction of special schools in residential locations. However, Stoll and Fink (1996: 133) observe:

> Schools can, as many do, isolate themselves to maintain control and avoid criticism.

The rhetoric of relations with the community is ambiguous. On the surface, it seems to relate to citizenship, public ownership, democratization and participation. It purports to empower consumers by making schools more accountable, while reducing professional and expert power. The relationship with the community is the alliance of the market place, with providers strategically positioned in relationship to purchasers of the educational product. Links with the community take on a new meaning when issues of recruitment and economic survival are at stake. David (1993: 2) indicates how:

> The Right argues that parents should be afforded the freedom to choose schools in an educational marketplace. Their demands will then improve educational standards. Schools which are not chosen by a group of parents will go out of business.

This implies a type of 'Darwinian selection' (Levacic, 1993: 176) in which schools that fail to improve their standards will fail to attract students, become financially unviable and close. The logic here is that the closure of the worst schools will raise average standards. A market culture implies volatility. Levacic (1993: 185) maintains that 'a market has to be dynamic – some producers flourish and grow while others decline or cease to trade'. This means that there is a resultant hierarchy of winners and losers. The social value of community can be undermined by marketization. Watkins (1994: 340) claims that market values of education are in opposition to notions of community:

> The commodification of education into a good which can be bought and sold just like a bag of potatoes fosters a sense of isolation, with neither the seller nor the buyer being particularly concerned as to the social condition of their fellow human beings. In this process, the marketing of education privileges the 'self' over the 'community'. The construction of education consumers reinforces the capitalist centrepoint that individual consumption is of higher value than society's well-being.

Issues of selectivity, competitive entry and league tables have implications for community relations.

Summary

There have been three fundamental and interconnected strategies of control introduced into the public services in the last two decades. These involve:

- the principle of competition;
- performance management and monitoring;
- the creation of operationally decentralized units, with simultaneous increase in centralized control, or decentralized centralization (Hoggett, 1996: 9).

Political objectives have been achieved, in part, by the establishment of a managerial ethic in education, as in other public services. School effectiveness is a legitimating methodology. Professional meaning and purpose have been framed by the performance culture. Some of the key changes have been, as follows:

- there are now powerful normative control strategies;
- success is judged by results and outcomes;
- the value base of education has shifted from welfare to market principles;
- the consumer has replaced the citizen, with the accompanying rhetoric of empowerment, community participation and choice.

While consumerism can be perceived as a refreshing challenge to state monopolies and archaic bureaucracies, and to the 'organisational indifference' (Hall, 1974) of mass public services, the market in education can operate as a class strategy. The construction of social actors as consumers stands in contradiction to any notion of community. Effectiveness has to be managed, measured and monitored in order for schools to maintain their positions in competitive market economies. While accountability is an important aspect of democracy, signifiers of educational performance have been reduced and schools have been forced into elaborate procedures for impression management. New managerialism, with its taxonomies and success criteria appears to enhance school effectiveness and efficiency. However, the chaos it purports to regulate is simply being sent underground in the form of failing schools, teacher stress and disaffection, and further social exclusion.

Questions
1   What are the central components of new managerialism? How have these been applied to school effectiveness?
2   Multiskilling is now a key concept in employment. To what extent do you believe that teachers should be managers too?
3   What are your views on community participation in education?

Chapter 5

Systems Maintenance: The New School Improvement Paradigm

The concept of school improvement has a long history with origins in different theoretical and ideological frameworks from those that have traditionally framed the school effectiveness paradigm. This chapter locates the evaluative basis of educational change and development during the 1960s and 1970s and highlights its grounding, historically, in a process of reflexive institutional change. This discussion is followed by an examination of the shifts in meanings that have taken place in the conceptualization of school improvement in the aftermath of the 1988 Education Act.

A View from the Past

During the 1960s and 1970s educational change and development revolved largely around the need to redress social class and linguistic inequalities – and, later, gender and 'racial' inequalities (see Chapters 1 and 7). The question as to why schools and schooling benefited some pupils and not others, provided a central point around which views about teaching and learning were articulated at the time. Framed by theories of disadvantage, equality of opportunity and social justice, emphasis then was on improving pupils' lifechances through a more equitable distribution of resources and knowledge. The idea of school improvement, to a significant extent, revolved around a philosophical re-appraisal of pedagogy. Influenced by the Plowden Report (1967), the ascendancy of cognitive psychology in education, and academic research into classroom teaching practices and learning processes (see, for example, Barnes et al., 1969; Barnes and Todd, 1977; and Edwards and Furlong, 1978), teachers were inducted into experiential, process-oriented learning, which positioned the child at the centre of the education process. Within the broader framework of comprehensive education, emphasis was placed on learning through group interaction in mixed-ability classes. This involved changes in the way that the curriculum was organized, teachers' views of the teaching and learning process and the context in which they taught.

James Callaghan's Ruskin College speech (1976) with its emphasis on improving educational standards and teacher accountability, signified an ideological break with welfare interventionism (see Chapter 2). This was consolidated in the Green Paper *Education in Schools: A Consultative Document* published in July 1977 and the Taylor Committee's Report (1977) *A New Partnership for Our Schools*. Within the changing climate in education during the late 1970s, attention shifted towards institutional development within the framework of systems theory. Operating within an input-process-output model, systems theory centres on *process* involving the inter-relationship between people, sub-systems within the organizational structure, technology (resources) and work tasks (Owens, 1991). Problems identified within structures, practices and processes are to be resolved systematically according to specified sets of criteria, which define desired outcomes. Within this paradigm school improvement relies on a variety of mechanisms such as whole-school policies, management strategies, staff training, monitoring, evaluation and target-setting in school development plans, staff appraisal, action research and, more recently, the notion of research and development (R & D). The notion of R & D derives from the redefined technological production model adopted in manufacturing industry since the 1980s (see Chapter 3).

Whole-School Policies: Radicalizing Possibilities and Ambiguities in School-Based Development

Of these mechanisms, whole-school policies constituted an important aspect of the management of planned change within schools during the early 1980s. This followed the systems approach advocated in the Hargreaves (1984) and Bullock Reports (1975). Other major influences were national and local education authority sponsored staff development projects focused on second language teaching and multicultural education. These emerged within organizations such as:

- the National Association for the Teaching of English (NATE);
- the Centre for Urban Educational Studies (CUES);
- initiatives within the Inner London Educational Authority (ILEA);
- the Schools Council National Writing Project; and
- the National Oracy Project.

Much of the research taking place in some of these projects was practice-oriented and played a considerable role in focusing teachers' attention on learning conditions in schools and classrooms (see also Skilbeck, 1984; Stenhouse, 1975). During the period 1981–8, whole-school policies were integrally linked with staff development on both a formal (e.g. linked with LEA in-service policies and provision) and informal (e.g. in-school working parties) basis. School-based working parties and subject-workshops allowed teachers to share ideas and to collaborate in the planning of teaching and learning. Inter-subject working parties focusing on cross-curricular issues contributed significantly to the breaking down of subject-barriers (see Hickman and Kimberley, 1988). Influences from research emphasizing the importance of building links between home and school, and pastoral education, contributed to a further breaking down of barriers between schools and the communities that they served (Marland, 1974; Lang and Marland, 1985; Craft et al., 1980). In some schools, these developments had a major influence on changing curriculum organization, teaching approaches and the general ethos in which teaching and learning took place (see Hickman and Kimberley, 1988).

In providing the principles that frame the teaching and organization of different subjects, and also the hidden curriculum, whole-school policies serve the purpose of identifying a common approach to teaching and learning within the school. As we argued in Chapter 4, the hidden curriculum refers to the norms, rules, behaviours, assumptions, expectations, values and ethos, interactions, the symbols and rituals that together constitute individual school culture. Arrived at through negotiation and co-operative decision making, whole-school policies generally reflect a shared vision of development, which binds teachers within a particular school together around a common identity as well as ways of knowing and ways of doing. Thus, they play a significant role in shaping the formal culture of the school.

At the same time, it is important to point out that despite the apparent consensus, whole-school policies have traditionally existed in tension since what constitutes organizational culture comprises significantly *more* than the overt and hidden curriculum. Organizational culture extends to differentiated patterns of human behaviour, different ideological and political positions, differential locations within the organizational hierarchy, alternative world views, and often also contradictory modes of conduct. Thus it includes individual values, aspirations and expectations that may not necessarily coincide with the normative meanings inscribed into the formal culture of the school. Teachers bring to the implementation process their own sets of values, biases, understandings and expectations. This accounts for some of the unintended outcomes of specific developments within individual organizations as became evident in the implementation of various policy initiatives in different schools at the time. For example, Ball's (1987) case study of Beachside Comprehensive School, illustrates the extent to which the move towards mixed-ability teaching was problematic in schools where teachers adhered to different ideologies of teaching and learning. As can be seen below, other school-based developments were to encounter similar difficulties in their implementation.

The general significance of these developments was the fact that in some schools, teachers during the early 1980s were engaged in defining their own development purposes that were given *voice* in whole-school policies. In many instances, this provided teachers with the possibility of challenging oppressive cultural meanings constructed around gender, 'race' and language (Rassool, 1995). It also enabled them to define discursive teaching as well as personal and professional learning purposes reaching beyond the functional and instrumental foci of human capital theory advocated by Harold Wilson and John Vaizey during the 1960s (see Chapters 1 and 2). For example, the emergence of community schools during the early 1980s, especially in some urban areas, resulted in adults attending mainstream lessons, and parents and the wider community being used as additional sources of support (see Hickman and Kimberley, 1988). Supported by LEA funding, the latter included providing teachers of community languages and translation services in schools with a high in-take of second language learners, or adult support for pupils with literacy difficulties. In this sense, the school and members within local communities could work towards self-defined common purposes; drawing on local literacies and knowledges. Many of these initiatives allowed teachers in some schools to appropriate key aspects of the equality of opportunity debate and re-interpret them in the interests of the particular needs of pupils within their schools. And thus they were enabled to fracture the normative rules, behaviours and expectations inscribed into formal schooling.

It could be said that in addressing through their subjects issues related to social class, disability, gender and 'racial' inequalities, and working in close relationship with communities beyond the school, teachers at the time were able to shape their own self-identities as practitioners. The concept of self-identity here derives from Giddens (1991) and refers to the discursive self engaged in an ongoing process of reflective and reflexive change, redefining their experience of the social world in terms of their particular understandings and discursive knowledges of that world and, in the process, creating different political, social and educational possibilities. Linked with debates within the broader social terrain, and with activism within specific social movements, it enabled the discursive world to be brought into the classroom. In other words, in some schools teachers were engaged in defining their own teaching and learning purposes in relation to the particular needs of specific groups of pupils within their schools. They also defined their development priorities in terms of the issues that prevailed in school, and the relationship between this and wider society and culture (see Hickman and Kimberley, 1988).

At the same time, however, this is not to argue that we can generalize about the nature of the changes that took place in schools at the time. Many of these local developments were riven with contradictions and ambiguities, and in some instances, gave rise to power struggles between different interest groups within particular institutions and communities. For example, in the case of multicultural education, the funding of community projects resulted in competition for resources between various community interest groups. Organizational cultures constituted in tension also contributed the problematic implementation of multicultural, anti-racist and special educational needs policies in some schools where staff were often divided into oppositional ideological camps.

The general points that we want to make here are that:

1   The general climate in education at the time provided possibilities for self-defined change.
2   This enabled teachers in some schools to engage as cultural workers and agents of change.
3   The parameters of school development were extended to include the communities in which particular schools were situated.
4   Whole-school policies provided an important mechanism in this process of locally defined change and development.

A systemic problem of whole-school policy initiatives during the early 1980s, ironically, lay in the fact that they did not form part of a coherent national policy approach that created the conditions for evaluation and change, and which provided national guidelines that could be adapted to local conditions. Instead, the nature of change and development that took place in individual schools depended greatly on the views and development priorities of LEAs, headteachers and other senior members of staff. Thus, it was that some schools were able to develop a coherent approach to teaching and learning based on the specific conditions within their schools and communities. Some of this included the provision of in-class curricular support for second language learners and pupils with special educational needs. In others, limited or no change took place.

Furthermore, self-empowering approaches, because they often engage in counter-hegemonic practices – and evolve within minority-interest sites – tend to have low currency in mainstream politics. And thus they always remain vulnerable to the political exigencies of the time. Anti-racist educational policy and practice challenged racial discrimination and addressed issues related to social justice and racial inequality. As such, it was confrontational: it contested prevailing practices. In response, the Conservative New Right discredited progressive educational approaches, and multicultural/anti-racist education which they argued constituted the politicization of education (see Chapter 2). The general effect of this was a gradual subjugation of the professional knowledges and expertise that teachers had acquired during the preceding decade. This referred, particularly, to the development of whole-school policies related to the context in which teaching and learning were taking place, and the teaching of critical knowledges. Within the new ethos, in-school evaluations of curriculum content and organization in relation to issues of equity in education centred on gender, 'race', second language learning and special needs education were curtailed. The silencing of teachers' collective voices, and the erosion of possibilities for self-defined innovation were to be secured in the 1988 Education Reform Act (ERA). Imposing a new framework and terms of reference on education, the ERA redefined the whole terrain of struggle and debate in education (Ball, 1990). Relinquished of their role as cultural workers, teachers became situated as functionaries within an increasingly technocratic educational context centred on the development of schools as 'expert' quality systems.

The New School Improvement Paradigm

Within the market-dominated post-ERA milieu with its emphasis on quality control and the regulation of teachers and teaching, the 'why' of school improvement has been replaced by 'what', 'when' and 'how' according to pre-determined standardized national criteria. Rather than constituting a self-defining process of development, the homogenized (and homogenizing) school improvement discourse that has developed since 1988, to a large extent, represents a reaction to external, centralized, forces. DiMaggio and Powell (1983) refer to this process of organizational homogenization as 'coercive isomorphism' which, they argue, arises when 'powerful forces emerge that lead (diverse organizations) to become more similar to one another' (1983: 150, information in brackets added). Coercive isomorphism 'results from both formal and informal pressures exerted on organisations by other organisations upon which they are dependent and by cultural expectations within society within which organisations function' (DiMaggio and Powell, 1983: 150). To this effect:

1   the standardized knowledges of the National Curriculum;
2   the rigid regulatory criteria of OFSTED inspections;
3   the regimentation and 'gaze' of various national 'Task Forces';
4   the publication of national league tables, and relatedly;
5   competition between schools

have all contributed to the emergence of a nationally uniform systems approach to school improvement guided by the development, largely, of technical expertise grounded in market-based rationalities.

Ideologically, the market-orientated structures, practices and processes that inhere in the 1988 ERA, support the 'professionalization' of teachers in line with the skills and competencies, and the technocratic sensibility needed to function within the corporate environment that now defines the concept of the 'self-managing' school. The latter is seen as depending on 'high reliability' amongst its workforce in order to 'avoid systems failure'. By 'ensuring that innovations are reliably spread throughout the school' (Reynolds, 1996) schools can maintain a competitive edge within the (segmented) educational market. In the drive for excellence in schools, learning has become an exchangeable commodity and, as such, it constitutes a potent form of hegemonic cultural capital. That is to say, it represents that in which all teachers *must* participate in order to operate effectively within a high-risk, competitive educational market environment. As will be seen below, the nature of this learning is framed by a very particular view of educational development.

In the drive for quality and excellence, schools must now:

- engage in capacity-building in terms of effective leadership;
- develop the ability to recognize 'blocks' in the process of change;
- have the capability to identify means to overcome these;
- to 'self-correct'; and/or
- to map out the scope of change.

This can be seen as replicating the need to reduce the porosity (gaps) within the work process in industry typified by the continuous improvement principles of *kaizen* described in Chapter 3. Processes including communication and decision making; information flows; co-ordination mechanisms such as the standardization of work processes, output, skills and knowledge; development planning; task allocation and supervision; and staff relationships are seen as being central to building 'the professional school culture' (Reynolds, 1996: 73).

Within an educational system defined by relentless policy-driven pressure to change and innovate, it was to be only a matter of time before school improvement would be re-defined and incorporated into the school effectiveness framework. During the crisis that surrounded the implementation of the ERA, acquiring management capability, and the putting into place of quality control mechanisms became development priorities. Since that time, the focus has shifted steadily from concerns about national policy implementation and related development projects, to the need to build the capacity of schools to improve themselves and to empower all teachers within the school community (Hopkins et al., 1994). On the surface, this signifies an important move towards improving the conditions for teaching and learning in schools. Several school improvement approaches have been advanced, some of which are summarized below.

Facilitating Mechanisms, Regulation and Control

The *Improving the Quality of Education for All* (IQEA) Project, based at the University of Cambridge Institute of Education represents what Reynolds (1992: 142) refers to as a 'strategic school improvement project'. The overall emphasis of the IQEA project has been on working with schools (more than forty schools in East Anglia and Yorkshire were involved) to improve the processes of teaching and learning, and involved six tutor-consultants in guiding schools in developing their capacity to improve. Looking at the *management* conditions necessary for school improvement during the early 1990s, the IQEA project identified specific aspects for development. These included staff development, pupil, parent and governor involvement, leadership, co-ordination and communication as well as collaborative planning (Hopkins, Ainscow and West, 1994; Beresford, 1996).

Apart from the accent on managerial leadership, this approach does not indicate a significant change from what has been considered to be good educational practice for at least the past 30 years. Certainly, the idea of the reflective and reflexive practitioner derives from earlier classroom-based action research conducted during the 1970s and 1980s (cf. Walker and Adelman, 1975; Elliott et al., 1979; Croll, 1986; Bell and Arnold, 1987). The concept also featured centrally in the critical pedagogy grounded in concrete problem solving advocated by Paulo Freire in adult education during the 1970s. The Freirean approach subsequently became influential also in mainstream education and, especially, in adult education. Collaborative teaching and learning, developing a shared teaching purpose, and goal-directed learning had formed the basis of 'progressivist' teaching approaches during the 1970s. This incorporation of meanings from a different socio-historical and ideological epoch into current frameworks serves to underline the significance of intertextuality in shaping educational development. In this regard, the school improvement debate seemingly has come full circle. What is different though is that the linguistic categories of description, and the progressivist philosophical and self-empowering pedagogical principles that had underpinned these teaching approaches during the 1970s and early 1980s, have now been neutralized within a 'de-ideologized' corporate educational context. Staff development has become organization-oriented, content-less and socially and culturally decontextualized.

What is interesting also is the extent to which the redefined integrated school effectiveness/school improvement discourse swings with the political times. In contrast to previous emphases on certainties of measurement Reynolds (1996: 104), for example, now adopts a more relativistic position. He argues that 'outcomes appropriate for measurement in the 1980s, such as academic achievement or examination attainment, may not be the only outcomes appropriate for the 1990s, where new goals concerning knowledge of "how to learn" or ability in mastering *(sic)* information technology may be necessary'. What is absent from his pragmatic formulation are both a pedagogic and philosophic rationale for this shift in focus.

The 'Learning School' and Organizational Theory

Another school improvement approach advocated revolves around the idea that schools, like their counterparts in business and industry, need to become 'learning' organizations. The learning organization thesis advanced by Schon (1983, 1967), Argyris and Schon (1996) and Senge (1990) is much cited in school improvement literature. The concept of the learning organization revolves around developing 'strategy, values, views of its environment, and understandings of its own competences' (Argyris and Schon, 1996: xxvii) in order to make the organization more effective in terms of output (productivity gains and increased profits), efficient in terms of work process, and also cost-effective. Understanding the culture, communication and interaction within the organization define the learning system. Aiming to identify problems within the organization in order to self-correct, the learning process entails changing ways of thinking, seeing and acting by involving people within the organization in reflective inquiry. As we will argue below, this reflection runs the risk of being self-referential and limited to the development of operational competencies.

Allowing for potential difficulties, Argyris and Schon (1996: xxvii) support a dual approach since, they argue, 'some kinds of learning take place within existing systems of values and action frames in which values are embedded (single-loop learning based on existing consensus), while other kinds involve changes in values and frames and call for reflective inquiry based on reflective inquiry that cuts across incongruent frames (double-loop learning based on potential conflict)' (information in brackets added). To this end, they advance a collaborative action-research approach that combines 'individual and interpersonal inquiry, and their underlying theories-in-use, to patterns of productive and unproductive learning (within the organization) at higher levels of aggregation' (Argyris and Schon, 1996: xxv). This approach offers a significantly different view of reflexivity to that which featured in whole-school policy initiatives during the early 1980s discussed above. In that context the impetus for change and development often related also to issues that evolved *beyond* the confines of the school. During that particular period, school improvement derived from a discursively constructed critical knowledge base. Here the school is presented as a hermetically sealed unit decontextualized from its wider social base. Moreover, it does not engage with the complex power and human relations in which organizational cultures are constituted. An important point to make is that although the concept of the 'learning' organization is often cited in the redefined school improvement paradigm, the literature does not generally *engage* with organizational theory and its limitations within the educational context; it merely provides the *rationale for change*.

The 'Learning' School and Continuous Improvement

In contrast to the complexity of argument that surrounds the concept of the learning organization including the ambiguities, paradoxes, contradictions and the control inherent in normative formulations, the notion of the 'learning' school is taken at a taken-for-granted face value. Learning is content-less and is defined in terms of:

1 Knowledge **or** learning *about* things.
2 Skills, Abilities, Competences **or** learning to *do* things.
3 Personal Development **or** learning to *become ourselves, to achieve our full potential*.

4   Collaborative Enquiry **or** learning to achieve things together. (Aspinall and Pedler, 1996: 230, emphasis original)

Stressing the importance of collaborative team work, Fullan (1993: 42) talks about the need to transform 'the school from a bureaucratic organisation to a thriving community of learners'. That is to say, schools need to develop a common identity and a common purpose. However, this argument loses sight of the fact that within the post-ERA context, the purpose of schools is defined largely by external centralized agents which constitute teachers as subjects to be monitored according to standardized sets of criteria. Forging a common purpose and identity in these circumstances would necessarily be circumscribed by existing structures.

Key characteristics of a 'learning' school include:

- a commitment to lifelong learning for all those within the school;
- an emphasis on collaborative learning and the creative and positive use of difference and conflict;
- a holistic understanding of the school as an organization;
- strong connections and relationships with the community and world outside the school. (Aspinall and Pedler, 1996: 240)

Other formulations of the characteristics of the 'learning' school include:

- the focus is on the pupils and their learning;
- individual teachers are encouraged to be continuing learners themselves;
- teachers (and sometimes others) who constitute the 'staff' are encouraged to collaborate by learning with and from each other;
- the school (all those people who constitute the school) learns its way forward, i.e. the school as an organization is a 'learning system';
- the headteacher is the leading learner. (Southworth, 1994: 53)

Graded in levels from one to five these categories frame the importance of children's learning, teacher learning, staff learning, organizational learning and leadership learning as integral aspects of the 'learning school' (Southworth, 1994). This framework does include a focus on children's learning, which is largely absent from other formulations. We return to a consideration of pedagogy later.

Despite their relative strengths, the frameworks presented here nevertheless share commonalities with the Japanese concept of continuous improvement embedded in the philosophical principles of *kaizen* described in Chapter 3. Grounded in the ideological practices and processes of managerialism, and subjected to the centralized 'gaze' of OFSTED and 'Task Force' surveillance, this idea of school improvement loses its potential for organic, self-defined change and development.

Schools are also categorized in terms of being either 'learning impoverished/ stuck' or 'learning enriched/moving' (Rosenholtz, 1989). Altering the climate within the school and developing 'collegiality' feature as necessary requisites for effecting a 'learning enriched or moving' school. The concept of 'collegiality', however, is not generally theorized and features in common-sense terms. In sociological terms, the concept of collegiality suggests the existence of structures that effect formal autonomy, formal procedures, self-regulation, an egalitarian peer-evaluation and informal control. Within the rigid structures put into place by the ERA and the central regulatory framework of current educational policy, such a concept of collegiality would seem to be somewhat misplaced in the present climate.

Within the 'learning' school paradigm schools are represented in anthropomorphic terms. Thus they need to *develop the capacity to learn*. It is believed that the better schools are at learning the more able they would be to detect and correct errors, and to address mismatches between intentions and outcomes. The nature of this learning is primarily competence-based and subscribes to the TQM practices discussed in Chapter 3, and thus it assumes compliance and/or consensus. Moreover, it does not take account of the argument in organizational theory that:

> organizational learning depends on the interpretation of events, which depends, in turn, on frames, the major story lines through which organiza-tional inquirers set problems and make sense of experience. Framing is essential to interpretive judgments, but because frames themselves are unfalsifiable, organizational inquirers may be trapped within self-referential frames. (Argyris and Schon, 1996: 197)

Our analysis bears out our earlier argument that formulations of the 'learning school' derive from a variety of technicist frameworks and, as such, they can be seen as representing a pastiche of eclectic assertions. These categories of description and the taxonomies that they underwrite, lack depth and a theoretically informed pedagogic and philosophical rationale. As it stands, the notion of the 'learning' school remains under-theorized. In assuming a generalized view of schools as being equivalent to business enterprises, it ignores the important role of schools as sites of cultural reproduction.

Effects, Impacts and Implications

What then are the implications of the current school improvement/school effectiveness paradigm for educational development generally? What are the effects of this formulaic and labour intensive approach to school improvement on the professional and personal lives of teachers? What opportunities are there for alternative ways of school development? To this end we need to step back and take a meta-perspective of the ideological framing of school improvement as well as the meanings that underpin classroom and school-based research and development.

Our interpretation indicates, first, an overall move in school improvement towards context-specific concerns within pre-defined conceptual frameworks that are circumscribed by centralized quality control mechanisms. Thus they demarcate the range of issues to be addressed, and the range of questions that can be asked. This rigid framing of development precludes a consideration of the wider picture in education including the relationship between education, culture and society within which the role of teachers and educational practice ultimately obtain their meaning.

Second, in analysing the concept of the 'learning' school we can discern patterns emerging that coincide with work processes associated with new production regimes. Integrating classroom research and teacher development into school development plans, can be seen as linking intertextually with earlier progressive educational approaches. However, grounded in the quality control ethos of production they can also be seen as representing the continuous improvement process of *kaizen* and the ideology of *companyism/ kaisha* discussed in Chapter 3. Developing a shared vision and shared meanings through inquiry and reflection within this context, fulfils the purpose of collecting what Garahan and Stewart (1992) refer to as company-specific 'parcels of knowledge' shared in *kaizen* meetings within the Nissan workplace. Organizational learning thus becomes 'an apparatus of surveillance and control (of labour) that by definition excludes the *framework* for other world views' (Garahan and Stewart, 1992: 77, information in brackets added). Moreover, in the leadership role associated with individual development projects as is advocated within the IQEA framework above, teachers can be seen to occupy the position of informal line managers supervising and co-ordinating the labour process within each development sphere. As such it constitutes a self-regulating technology.

Third, these meanings are also framed by educational policy. In the crusade for excellence identified in the New Labour White Paper *Excellence in Schools* (1997), school improvement will increasingly be defined in terms of 'benchmarking' by the School Effectiveness Unit (SEU). Grounded in the concept of continuous improvement, benchmarking is seen as providing an objective means of identifying 'best practice'. In industry, benchmarking serves to 'support the value creation process, to prioritize opportunities for improvement, enhance performance against customer expectations and to leapfrog the traditional cycle of change' (McNair and Leibfried, 1992: 18). It focuses on strategic planning and management involving short- and medium-term operational aims revolving around the effectiveness and efficiency of processes, services and roles and functions of particular people within the organization. As is argued by McNair and Leibfried (1992: 24) 'the purpose is to generate action, some form of improvement, that will enhance the value of the organization to its stakeholders'. Benchmarking already features in school improvement projects in which 'best practice' identified within departments provide the basis for quality management. Reynolds (1996: 140), for instance, advocates a context-specific approach to school improvement that involves auditing and 'the generation of knowledge about what to change at both an organisational and cultural level from scanning existing best practice within the school, in other schools and from the research literature'. This reflects the move towards organizational isomorphism discussed earlier. It also reflects the continuous improvement embedded in the *kaizen* and TQM practices discussed in Chapter 3. Making available examples of 'best practice' through the development of a national database, and the reliance on performance data will secure the 'policy of zero tolerance of underperformance' advocated in the White Paper (DfEE, 1997). Yet what is 'best practice' in one school may not necessarily transfer to another context, and thus the relentless pressure for improvement may not necessarily contribute to meaningful change. The policy of zero-tolerance of underperformance may exact unnecessary change at a high human cost in schools.

Fourth, learning together, or collaboratively, or creating a community of learners, as is suggested in the reformulated school improvement discourse, is a laudable aim and an achievement in education generally. However, the tension between pursuing individual and communal aims/personal and institutional development is a factor that needs to be taken into account in discussions on school improvement. The location of these concepts within the rigid framework of the school development plan needs to be seen in terms of the important ideological functions that it serves. It provides:

- the synergy through which individuals working together can accomplish more than they could alone and helps to build a corporate identity and solidarity;
- the means by which individuals 'learn that personal contributions to the development of the labour process must be carefully tailored and articulated in a company-sanctioned discourse' (Garahan and Stewart, 1992: 103);
- the means *par excellence* through which teachers are incorporated into a totalizing quality control process; and
- it serves to ratify the idea of continuous learning through which 'people continually expand their capacity to create the results they truly desire . . . and are continually learning to learn together' (Senge, 1990, quoted in Koteen, 1997: 328). Self-monitoring and the implicit 'neighbourhood-check' by colleagues approach does not allow for individual interpretations, innovation, alternative practices and different possibilities. The self and mutual gaze is all encompassing.

Fifth, we need to examine the substantive knowledge base of the 'learning school' and the particular forms of thinking and levels of involvement that it engenders. Senge et al. (1994), for example, identify five 'technologies' necessary in the learning organization. This includes *systems thinking* which is focused on detecting problems and consequences, exploiting opportunities, and rapidly mobilizing information and expertise for solutions. *Personal mastery* encourages lifetime learning and seeks to enhance the affective requirements of development. *Mental models* refer to familiar ways of thinking that may serve as an inhibitor of development by influencing what we do and how we act. This is overcome by questioning the assumptions and hidden motives that people bring with them to the change process and redefining them in the interest of the organization's development. *Shared vision* is seen as a key aspect of the learning organization and central to strategic planning in terms of developing a corporate image of the future, a code of values, mission and achievable aims. *Team learning* is seen as vital in terms of developing insight into complex problems within a context of rapid change, the need to innovate, and co-ordinated action and co-operative decision making through dialogue. Such a labour intensive approach through which the individual becomes fully incorporated into the organization, if transferred to education, leaves little room for reflection beyond operational and instrumental concerns within individual schools. In this regard, the devolution of INSET funding to schools could serve to reinforce the development of local school-based (company-based) skills.

Appraisal: Self-Monitoring, Accountability and Target-Setting

The notion of workers' self-accountability, and their accountability to the 'firm' also feature centrally in the appraisal process. Teacher appraisal involves peer evaluation of professional achievements that, in turn, are evaluated in relation to how effectively they meet the objectives of the School Development Plan (SDP). Targets set in terms of the improvement of skills and performance, in turn, are linked with the global targets set around the resource framework and policy objectives identified in the SDP (DES Circular, 12/91).

Within this circumscribed framework, teacher appraisal is caught up in the process-oriented exigencies of the school as a self-functioning unit with no real relationship with the overall career development of teachers beyond the immediate confines of the specific institution. Thus it can be seen as representing a predominantly production-led, employer validated, and controlled, process of incremental or continuous improvement. Far from empowering teachers in relation to their overall development, depending on individual institutions' interpretations of and meanings attached to the appraisal process, it can be seen as serving to imbue them with a self-monitoring and self-regulating consciousness. Teacher appraisal can then be seen to have much in common with the shaping of teacher subjectivities rather than with the generic skill and career empowerment of teachers as professionals.

There appear to be tacit correspondences between the principles of teacher appraisal and the concepts of both 'companyism' and, tied to the concept of continuous professional development, it also shares commonalities with the concept of *kaizen*. Appraisal meetings can be seen as providing the equivalent of peer assessment in *kaizen* meetings whilst simultaneously incorporating individual workers into the instrumental aims and ethos of the institution.

Chasing 'quality targets' set in line with SDP objectives can also be viewed as providing a means of identifying both overall team – and individual – achievements whilst at the same time, highlighting whole areas of weakness, or individual shortcomings. Linked with possibilities for career advancement within the institution, it represents a powerful means of 'promoting individual competition' (Garahan and Stewart, 1992: 108). This is especially important if viewed in relation to the prospect of headteachers' discretion in deciding performance-related pay supported in the Green Paper *Teachers – Meeting the Challenge of Change* (DfEE, 1998) – and its ultimate consolidation of core and periphery workers within the education system. At the same time, it can also limit the expectations and motivation of teachers in terms of their personal development goals.

Pedagogy: Empowerment, Justice and Equity

We have argued throughout this chapter that we need to view the integrated school effectiveness/school improvement paradigm in relation to the overall ideological and conceptual framework in which it operates. As we have seen, quantitative performance data remain key aspects of school improvement discourses. These also feature prominently in the White Paper *Excellence in Schools* (1997) as indicators of pupil progress as well as school and subject performance on a national level. As a key quality control variable, performance data now serve an important means of identifying 'failing' schools and, relatedly, to define 'Fresh Start' options, and also to 'promote "hallmarked" models and standards for school self-evaluation' (DfEE, 1997: 33). In the crusade for quality and effectiveness, performance data play an important role in identifying the winners and losers; separating the 'blue chip' from those to 'go into liquidation'. Seemingly then, social Darwinism has re-entered educational policy discourse. Ironically, it is not guaranteed that the survivors would necessarily be the best practitioners.

Representatives of the 'third wave' of school improvement have started to highlight the need to shift emphasis from concerns about school development to classroom conditions for learning (Creemers, 1994; Southworth, 1996). This, it is argued, is especially important in primary schools where the class teacher exercises great influence over the learning process. Enhancing the skills and knowledge of teachers therefore represents an important aspect of teacher development. Recent concerns about pedagogy and teachers' professional development have been influenced by views expressed within the Teacher Training Agency (TTA) about the need for continuous professional development (CPD) and the development of national standards for key points in the profession (Southworth, 1996). It is also an important focus of OFSTED school inspections. Pedagogy is thus interpellated with teaching quality which is, largely, undefined and tied to specific sets of functional meanings centred on a normative effectiveness.

Collaborative planning engendered by the need to organize National Curriculum teaching, and its relationship with the school development plan is seen as having fostered a culture of interdependence in schools, and particularly, primary schools. New emphases are placed on classroom action research, classroom observation, team teaching, demonstrations of good classroom practice, staff conferencing on individual pupils, monitoring pupils' work and analysis of pupil outcome data (Southworth, 1996). That these aspects are central to developing teachers' professional knowledge is not disputed; it is the broader *purposes* and *ends* that they serve that are important. As we argued earlier, these developments do not represent any significant change to what has been considered good school practice at least since the early 1980s. The difference is that during the early 1980s, these approaches were framed by philosophical views on teaching and learning grounded in the principles of inclusion, creative problem-solving and process learning focused on the development of the child as a whole. Within the redefined general educational framework they serve primarily as a means towards increasing measurable output quality. Pedagogy is defined loosely in terms of 'core tasks' such as the structure of teaching sessions, planning, questioning techniques, clarity of instructions, use of praise, feedback, teachers expecta- tions of pupils, and grouping strategies. Focused on the 'how' of teaching, this view of pedagogy centres primarily on the operational aspects of teaching defined in terms of teachers' packages of 'craft knowledge'. Combined with the notion of collaborative learning embedded in the concept of the 'learning' school, this shares similarities with the idea of on-the-job training integrated into work tasks, and the sharing of craft knowledges implicit in the process of *kaizen*, which involve workers in identifying techniques and approaches in the pursuit of 'quality targets'. Overall, it represents a linear input-output production model of teaching and learning.

What is absent from this view of pedagogy are the affective, ethical awarenesses and the substantive pedagogical knowledges needed to work with pupils. This includes the continuing development of teachers' understanding of teaching and learning processes; their knowledge of culture and the social world. Teachers need to understand the range of theories that underpin learning and, therefore, the pedagogical rationale for adopting different teach- ing approaches in different situations and with particular pupils. Professional development needs to extend to understanding the psychology of children's development, and the cognitive, cultural and socio-economic factors that prevent some pupils from having equal access to the full range of knowledges within the curriculum. This is especially important in the contemporary world in which a wide range of social factors such as unemployment, drug addiction, poverty and social dislocation now shape the everyday experiences of children in schools. Pedagogy, in other words, in addition to cognitive development, needs to engage also with the multi-layered aspects of social difference and, relatedly, the complexities that surround issues of equity in the modern world.

Pedagogy as represented in the post-ERA (and New Labour) school improvement paradigm, does not provide a view of children as active meaning-makers and the role of teachers as cultural workers. Ultimately, issues of pedagogy cannot realistically be defined outside a consideration of the ways in which structural and structured inequalities, violence, and the chaos in which contemporary social life is constituted, impact on teaching and learning in schools and classrooms. Pedagogy defined only in procedural and functional managerial terms, would serve to homogenize the diversity that constitutes classrooms and schools. Articulated, as it is, primarily around operational competencies, transmission and measurable standards, the prevailing school improvement paradigm denies the transformative potential of classroom activity.

Pedagogy also cannot be discussed outside a consideration of the social construction of knowledge within the curriculum; that the curriculum represents multi-vocal narratives situated in forms of representation and relations of power that legitimate particular views of what is knowledge and knowing within the culture. Thus it is constituted in multi-layered meanings. The view presented in the school improvement/school effectiveness paradigm does not include the negotiation of differential power relations within classrooms between teachers and pupils; between teachers as professionals, and in terms of what is taught, how and why. Rather, the curriculum is treated as a closed system, a social, cultural and educational 'given' to be implemented in a technical way.

Embedded in a *mea culpa* sensibility, and a deficit model of development, the view of pedagogy in the school effectiveness/school improvement framework has a limited perspective of the role of education in the modern world. It makes no allusions to the need to develop discursive ways of engaging with the changing learning conditions in the global cultural economy. Pedagogy, in other words, needs to be theorized in relation to not only content and process, but also social and cultural forms of knowledge, and discourse. The latter refers to the construction of meanings within and around the school as a cultural practice and its relationship with the curriculum and the classroom context.

Summary

Driven by the need for excellence in schools, organizational change and development is now circumscribed by national educational policy, and regulated by a diverse range of centralized, and devolved, regulatory mechanisms. Thus validated, the new integrated school effectiveness/school improvement discourse consolidates a normative representation of schools and schooling. In this teachers feature as functionaries in a linear input-output school process which relies predominantly on the acquisition and ongoing maintenance of procedural skills and techniques.

- it is primarily concerned about engendering an organizational culture grounded in normative procedures and performance management, and the creation of context-specific purposes and meanings;
- it also rationalizes a common value-system embedded in market principles, and a common, neutral representation of the world framed by rigid, homogenizing sets of taxonomies and target-setting;
- it implies a normative unity of purpose and outcome despite local differences;
- combined with the limited focus on organizational explanations of cause and effect, it excludes a consideration of the multi-realities of the pupils represented in the schools and their discursive relationship with socially produced (and reproduced) inequalities;
- compared to its previous links with self-identification and self-definition, the concept of teacher empowerment has been neutralized within a site-based process of continuous improvement.

Thus it serves to ratify a linear procedural technicism and a technocratic professional consciousness.

Questions
1 What is a systems approach to school improvement?
2 What is your understanding of the concept of 'the learning organization'?
3 What advantages and disadvantages do you see in relation to:
   (a) school development plans
   (b) target setting
4 How would you define pedagogy?

Chapter 6

The Irrationality of School Effectiveness in Developing Countries

The technology of school effectiveness now constitutes a major UK export commodity on a global scale. Tailor-made courses, and their accompanying software, packaged and delivered by external educational consultants, offer practical business solutions to seemingly intractable educational problems in developing countries. Technical 'know-how' thus injected into the management structures and processes of educational systems ostensibly fulfils the important function of 'adjusting' and 'revitalizing' schools and, in the process, making them more functionally effective, efficient and cost-effective. To a large extent, this reflects the internationalization of market forces ideology that now underpins educational policy in industrialized countries. This refers, especially, to the principles of new managerialism as the expedient means through which systemic change is managed and maintained. It also highlights the important role that international funding agencies such as the World Bank and the International Monetary Fund (IMF) play in the shaping of educational development priorities in different parts of the world.

We argue in this chapter that whilst the technical-rational solutions offered to educational problems in developing countries reflect global economic policy shifts during the 1980s, issues about quality in education within these societies are more complex and have roots in both colonial rule and post-colonial national development. We examine the impact that the protracted period of colonialism had on educational practices and provision in terms of:

- the general resourcing of schools;
- the differential levels to which education was made available to various social groups in these societies;
- the important role that the organization of schooling, and the ideological framing of curriculum knowledge played in the shaping of societal relations.

We argue that the legacy of historical inequalities contributed to a significant extent to the fact that many post-colonial countries started their development with an inadequate educational infrastructure. Post-colonial development policies during the 1960s provided the context in which national aspirations were shaped around the role of education in stimulating economic growth whilst, at the same time, developing a national consciousness. As can be seen in the discussion below, in many post-colonial countries, education also provided the primary means by which the ideology of nationalism was introduced into the body politic. We explore the long-term impact of post-colonial development policies on educational provision.

One of the main threads in this chapter revolves around the argument that although these epochs represent two distinctive periods in the histories of most developing countries, the transition from one milieu to another did not necessarily represent a clear ideological, political and cultural break. Residual cultural meanings, behaviours, processes and practices of colonialism are intertextually linked with those that evolved during the post-colonial period.

School Effectiveness as a Power/Knowledge Discourse

Contemporary analyses of school effectiveness in the international terrain (Lockheed and Verspoor, 1991; Levin and Lockheed, 1993; Lockheed, 1993), including those that adopt a critical stance (Harber and Davies, 1997), tend to use as their starting point the construction of the 'developing' world – and particularly Africa – as 'problem', as a linear 'truth'. Complex historical effects of societal development are reduced to, for example:

- the social pathology of endemic corruption;
- authoritarian states and autocratic leadership;
- cultural differences;
- the rise in social violence;
- high birth rate;
- rising school dropout rates;
- under-resourced schools;
- inadequate school buildings; and
- under-developed human resources.

These deficit development clichés feature as explanatory variables of under-development. In providing the categories of description which demarcate what can and should be said about education and development within developing countries, they serve to justify 'strategic' intervention in the form of external consultancies and aid programmes. In practice, these are not benign forms of intervention; they form part of the vast international aid-in-development industry.

The articulation of these taken-for-granted 'truths' from within key defining sites such as the World Bank, UNESCO, and academic research plays an important role in structuring international 'moral panics' around 'poverty levels', 'failing education systems', 'criminality and lawlessness' and 'freedom and democracy'. Implicit in this is the bi-polar notion of 'civilization' represented in the industrialized world as against the moral and social 'backwardness' of the developing or under-developed world. Framed by the languages of development experts, these discourses 'speak with authority, they legitimate and initiate practices in the world, they privilege certain visions and interests' (Ball, 1990: 22). Having diagnosed the scale and nature of the problem they proceed to offer idealized, 'scientific' solutions to what in practical terms, are complex societal problems. Thus these articulations are instrumental in structuring international 'norms' circumscribed by criteria formulated by those who have the power to define. In doing so, they serve to:

- construct particular views of reality;
- legitimate selective understandings of societal needs; and
- impose specific forms of development;

and their regulation within rigid, and externally imposed, monitoring and evaluative frameworks. In doing so, they often displace local ways of knowing and doing, knowledge and expertise and, in thus circumscribing possibilities of thought, they prevent the possibility of imagining alternative futures within these societies.

By making available 'truth' as perceived by those who have power and control, these articulations can be seen as constituting power/knowledge discourses *par excellence*. Tied in with specific aid-programmes, they engender a political culture that will demarcate the range of organizational, technical and societal choices that can be made in planning for educational development. But since 'under-development and inequality in the poorer countries cannot be ascribed simply to structural features or to the values, traditions, and beliefs of their population' (Bacchus, 1997: 3), these articulations do not tell the whole story. Nor do the 'smart' technicist knowledges that they subscribe to have the scope to offer real and lasting solutions to the complex educational needs in developing countries.

For whilst conditions of poverty, deprivation and mismanagement do prevail within many developing countries, they do not necessarily *explain* the different realities within these societies. They are the *effects* of complex historical factors and events that have, over long periods of time, shaped them. In recognizing and acknowledging these complexities it follows, therefore, that any solutions to the educational difficulties encountered within these societies must necessarily take account of how things came to be the way they are within particular contexts. That is to say, what are the political, cultural and economic factors that, historically, influenced the shaping of the 'social character' within different societies, helping some to succeed and others not? Williams (1961: 146) describes the 'social character' as relating to much more than behavioural norms and attitudes to include also 'the transmission of a particular system of values, in the field of group loyalty, authority, justice, and living purposes'(see also Chapter 3). What are the reasons for the high levels of school drop-out rates within some societies? Why do many of these countries have an under-developed social/educational infrastructure? Is this due only to mismanagement and inward looking national policies as is generally suggested in the school effectiveness/school improvement framework? How effectively do the solutions offered within the school effectiveness/school improvement paradigm relate to the current trajectory of under-development within these societies?

Colonial and Post-Colonial Realities: the Myth of Human Capital Theory

The 1960s represented the period when many developing countries emerged from their long history of colonialism towards post-colonial independence. For many countries, education played an important role in forging a new national identity as well as providing a route towards economic self-reliance. Whilst many post-colonial countries opted for centralized socialist models of governance, their development priorities were shaped by external influences ratified to a large extent in the funding processes of the World Bank, the International Monetary Fund (IMF), UNESCO and individual industrialized aid-donating countries. Supported by economic theories that prevailed at the time, the concept of social development was underpinned by the view that:

> complex social problems could be understood through systematic analysis and solved through comprehensive planning . . . They further believed that they could construct models or theories of social change to aid in problem definition and policy formulation, that the resulting policies would respond adequately to human needs, and that there was a direct relationship between government action and the solution of social problems'. (Rondinelli, 1993: 3–4)

Corporate rationalist approaches to social development employing 'cost-benefit analysis, linear programming models, network scheduling, and planning/programming/budgeting systems' (Rondinelli, 1993: 4) were adopted. These were then applied to the multi-levelled planning problems that beset emerging post-colonial societies.

Of significance was the widespread adoption during the 1960s of the accelerated economic growth model of development supported by the principles of modernization theory. With the overall emphasis on increasing the gross national product (GNP) through higher levels of productivity, educational priorities became defined generally in terms of maximizing the 'human capital' in society (see Chapter 2). This was the case despite the fact that the deficiency of this technicist input-output concept of development had already been illustrated in the economic realities that had existed during earlier periods. For example, during the period of colonialism the majority of the population were functionally illiterate, un- or under-educated and existed at the periphery of these societies. This was also the case with South Africa during the Apartheid regime which represented neo-colonialism by a settler class. In many colonial and neo-colonial societies, especially in Africa, mass education for indigenous population groups was not generally available beyond primary school level. According to Ball (1983: 251):

> In 1939 there was still no secondary education for Africans anywhere in Central Africa. This position was carefully sustained in Central and East Africa by a rigid racial segregation of schooling for the European settlers, the Indians and the Africans . . . In 1934 Morris, Director of Education in Uganda, closed four of the eight junior secondary schools in the Protector-ate because of what he saw as the consequences of the over-production of school graduates who would be the 'political emissaries of agitation and discontent' and have no outlet for their energies 'but political intrigue and the flouting of authority'.

Classroom over-crowding, and by that fact, high teacher-pupil ratios, shift teaching and a general scarcity of relevant textbooks, the exclusion of girls from education, non-enrolment as a result of poverty and the common use of child-labour, and under-qualified teachers were already then part of everyday reality in many schools, and especially in rural areas.

Jora Sol (1985: 26) describing his experiences of teaching in both British Colonial and Apartheid South Africa expressed the view that 'because there was a shortage of accommodation, schooling for many was accomplished on a "shift" system. This meant that there was extra pressure on books, classroom equipment and teachers as they were all used twice over'. Pupil-teacher ratio in black schools worked out at an average of 55 to 60:1. During the Apartheid years 82 per cent of teachers employed by the Bantu Education Administration had an education standard of Junior Certificate and below. In order to assist teachers in overcrowded classrooms, widespread use was made of the 'monitor' system. Although monitors were originally there to help with the cleaning of classrooms and assisting handicapped pupils, in the 'black homelands' they tended to be used as teachers (Jora Sol, 1985). Unqualified and under-qualified teachers already then were normal features in educational practice.

Educational quality with regard to both input and outcomes, did not constitute a significant variable in general considerations of economic and social development during the colonial epoch. Indeed, differential levels of access to particular forms of schooling and curricula for different population groups provided the means by which particular forms of economic growth could be stimulated. Widespread use of low or unskilled labour in agriculture and the mining industry, meant that capital growth could be stimulated with negligible investment in education for the disenfranchized population groups. Colonial educational policy supported a 'model of social development that required a subservient, under-educated population which would provide a rich source of unskilled and semi-skilled labour, with the exception of a core elite' (Rassool, 1999: 63). As is documented in the writings of the Kenyan author, Ngugi wa Thiongo (1993), differential levels of access to education also played an important role in structuring a stratified consciousness amongst different groups within society. Education played a central part in shaping and maintaining the hegemony of colonialism as much in the curriculum content, as it did in the ways that schooling was organized.

Yet, ironically, despite widespread lack of investment in education, productivity levels during both colonial and neo-colonial periods remained high, contributing to annual increases in the GNP. Colonial economies continued to flourish. This factor calls into question the links established between education and the development of human capital, and their collective impact on raised levels of productivity and economic growth.

Authoritarianism structured into the domination and subordination of oppressed groups is another legacy of colonial rule; it permeated every level of social life. Cecil Rhodes speaking on the 'native question' in South Africa during the nineteenth century, stated that:

> I will lay down my policy on the native question. Either you have to receive them on an equal footing as citizens or call them a subject race. I have made up my mind that there must be class legislation, that there must be pass laws and peace preservation Acts . . . We must adopt a system of despotism such as works so well in India in our relations with the barbarians of South Africa. (quoted in Jora Sol, 1985: 26)

Similar meanings were later to be inscribed into 'Bantu' education by Hendrik Verwoerd who championed the Apartheid Education Bills. Arguing for controls to be exercised over the nature and type of education that black population groups were to receive, Verwoerd expressed the view that:

> I have travelled through the Transkei and have found some excellent establishments where the natives are taught Latin and Greek . . . There are kafir parsons everywhere. They are turning into a dangerous class. That is why I say that regulations of these schools should be framed by the government, otherwise these kafir parsons would develop into agitators against the government (quoted in Jora Sol, 1985: 26 ['kafir' is a racist term used to describe black people]).

Quarterly conferences serving to disseminate detailed instructions on content, prescribed teaching methodologies and use of prescribed textbooks subsequently represented the means by which teachers became inducted into the Nationalist Party government's preferred ways of working.

School Effectiveness in Apartheid South Africa

School effectiveness taxonomies were already in place throughout South Africa during the 1960s, and became technically more refined during the 1970s when 'record books' systematically recording teachers' coverage of the syllabus, became the focal point of all teaching. Annual school inspections ensured a cost-effective as well as an efficiently functioning educational system. Library inspectors were appointed to monitor school libraries annually for 'contraband', that is, books that contained 'inaccurate' historical facts and had been banned by the government. Over and above this was the surveillance of teachers by police spies. Teachers who were reported to be teaching alternative views, or not following the curriculum rigidly were placed under 'house arrest' (which meant that they could not physically leave their homes or consort with more than two people at any one time), or were transferred hundreds of miles away from their homes. This shows the extent to which school-effectiveness taxonomies and surveillance practices were used by the neo-colonial government to exercise control over what was being taught, how this was taught, monitored and evaluated. As we have argued, taxonomies are not neutral, they represent the interests and priorities of powerful definers.

But within this super-efficient educational service, science teaching took place without laboratories and, as is argued above, shared textbooks became the primary source of learning. Moreover, farm schools (referred to colloquially as 'one-man' schools as they had one teacher [mostly male] who taught all age groups in one class) were funded by the Bantu Affairs Department (BAD) and the Coloured Affairs Department (CAD). These departments provided desks and a minimal supply of textbooks; parents had to pay for any additional requirements including all writing equipment and the school uniform (Jora Sol, 1985). In a situation where adult farm wages at the time averaged £8.00 per month, many did not send their children to school on a regular basis.

The point that we want to make is that because of the historical lack of spending on education, by the end of colonial and neo-colonial rule, many developing countries did not have a substantive educational infrastructure on which to build a policy of universal access to education. In practice it meant that post-colonial countries inherited a largely dysfunctional and uneven education system with vast inequalities between whole sectors of society. In countries such as Kenya and Tanzania, this included disparities structured during the period of colonialism between formal educational provision for a small elite urban group who would continue to benefit, whilst for others, especially those living in rural areas, the lack of infrastructure meant a continuation of inadequate levels of provision. Widespread under-funding of education was reflected also in inadequate school buildings, un- and under-qualified teachers as well as a general shortage of teaching and learning resources. Post-colonial states also inherited an authoritarian educational system which developed during the colonial period. Altogether the colonized had been disempowered through regimentation and a systematized process of social, economic, political and educational disenfranchizement.

Because of the unequal nature of the educational policies underwritten by colonial and neo-colonial regimes, countries redefining their development goals following independence had to contend with *historically under-funded educational systems*. They also had to contend with widespread societal poverty and a generally inadequate infrastructure to support health, housing and social welfare. In many countries the existing infrastructure was subsequently to be destroyed during years of civil war as was the case in Zimbabwe, and/or in power struggles between factional power-interest groups within various societies. Thus, whilst education nominally featured at the forefront of development priorities in most post-colonial societies during the 1960s (and is now the case in post-Apartheid South Africa), these often had to be balanced against diverse sets of social need, and also various political expediencies within the struggle for power in many of these societies.

Education and National Self-Definition: the Tanzanian Experiment

With much of the emphasis in the modernization paradigm on developing skills and knowledge to facilitate levels of productivity and, therefore, economic growth, the 1970s witnessed expansion in education in most post-colonial countries. An often cited success story is the post-Arusha policy of 'education for self-reliance' pursued within the ideological framework of *ujamaa* socialism by President Nyerere of Tanzania. Educational policy shaped around the idea of developing self-reliance was aimed at a complete systemic overhaul, and an ideological re-orientation of education within that country. In particular, it supported a transformation in teaching approaches throughout education from the erstwhile authoritarian approach towards generating an inclusive and democratic, self-empowering ethos in schools. In line with the principles of *ujamaa* socialism, classroom ethos was to alter towards transferring power from the teacher to the pupil by emphasizing active participative learning, problem solving and formative examinations. Moreover, 'examinations were to be downgraded in government and public esteem, and combined with teachers' assessments of "character" and "willing-ness to serve" in terms of school and community work' (Davies, 1990: 112–113). Quality, in this instance, was defined in terms of the contribution that education could make to the development of the community as a whole. Emphasis therefore was on maximizing the social returns of education.

Defining the ideology of 'education for self-reliance', Nyerere expressed the view that 'the first objective of adult education must be to shake ourselves out of a resignation to the kind of life Tanzanian people have lived for many centuries past. We must become aware of the things that we, as members of our human race, can do for ourselves and for our country' (quoted in Bhola, 1984: 141). Nyerere's mission included the desire to reshape the social character of the nation turning them from subjects into change agents rooted in self-definition. Schools were encouraged to teach self-reliance by providing for learning about agriculture in on-site school farms and participating in numerous community self-help projects.

Education for self-reliance was accompanied by a programme of political education and was organized within a centralized syllabus aimed at teaching primary school children (Standards 3–6) the principles of citizenship. In addition to developing their understanding of the liberation struggle and the principles of *ujamaa* socialism, the syllabus included inducting pupils into the ideology of the national party (Chama Cha Mapinduzi) which revolved around inculcating respect for the national flag, the nationalist party song, knowledge about national party leaders and the history of the party. Pupils learned their national anthem, and about their national currency, festivals and symbols such as the Uhuru (freedom) torch, the constitution, styles of leadership and elections (Harber, 1989). In other words, education for citizenship permeated the whole curriculum.

But, although revolutionary in its orientation, this concept of self-reliance ultimately served to legitimate the principles of production and entrepreneurism, which obtained legitimacy because of its support for independent subsistence within the community. As became evident in its high profile participation in the UNESCO funded Experimental Literacy Programme (EWLP) (1969–71), the country's economic development was fundamentally grounded in the principles of modernization. Underlying principles of modernization theory included the drive for rapid technological and scientific development in order to 'catch-up' with the already industrialized economies of the developed world. This approach was further supported by Rostow's (1966) stages of economic development theory which suggested that increased levels of education and higher levels of literacy, would stimulate economic development by raising the country's levels of scientific and technical knowledge. This was regarded as necessary prerequisites to countries reaching the 'take-off' stage of development. Higher levels of school attainment were to be 'directly related to modernity-linked orientations; the raising of educational and occupational aspirations, less adherence to traditional customs and beliefs, and an openness to new experiences' (Forojalla, 1993: 12–13).

Functional literacy, which integrated literacy skills acquisition with practical tasks in the workplace, provided the educational basis of this model of development in countries that participated in the EWLP, which focused predominantly on adult education. The need to modernize also became the rationale for extended investment in educational provision at primary school level. By 1976 Tanzania, as was the case with other countries such as Nigeria and Kenya, were providing universal primary education.

Nevertheless, despite increased levels of investment in education, Tanzania since that time has not benefited from an equal distribution of education across the various sections of society. Alongside the 'flag-waving' nationalism nurtured within the country, was the growing lack of textbooks and learning materials and a rapidly expanding and largely ineffective bureaucracy represented by the introduction of democratic school councils. There are still vast educational and economic disparities between urban educated groups and the rural illiterate poor. In relation to this, Rubagumya

(1990: 2) argues that 'education for self-reliance cannot be achieved by attaching to the school a token *shamba* (farm, garden) while the whole system is still geared to the selection of the few who will make it to the top'. Secondary school provision has not expanded during the past decade and for many pupils primary education is the sum total of the education that they will receive in their lifetimes. The colonial practice of boarding schools still prevails, catering for only a small elite group who can afford to send their children to school beyond the primary phase. With regard to teaching and learning, by the late 1970s and early 1980s not much had changed educationally in that most schools had remained authoritarian, classrooms still operated on the basis of rote-learning and copying of notes, and examinations still measured memorization rather than skills and understanding (Harber, 1989). In other words, old values prevalent during the colonial period still form part of the social character.

Planning Development and the Reshaping of Post-Colonial Economies: the Role of External Funders

Post-colonial industrialization throughout the developing world has been financed primarily by external capital borrowing, notably from the International Monetary Fund (IMF) and the World Bank, with many countries accruing national debt to the level of 38 per cent of their gross national product (GNP). Following the world recession in the aftermath of the OPEC 1973 crisis, most of the developing world was beset by the inability to repay their national debt, falling commodity prices and a decrease in export markets. During the 1980s World Bank loans were tied in with stringent controls through its Structural Adjustment Programme (SAP) in order to reduce imbalances, correct policy biases and to establish the basis for sustainable economic growth (Stewart, 1994). This included the adoption of market and price liberalization, monetarist fiscal policy, and currency devaluation to facilitate exports.

The fiscal policy advocated by the SAP demanding a decrease in public expenditure, has impacted catastrophically on educational provision in many developing countries. Enrolment rates have declined and basic teaching resources, especially books, pencils, chalk, maps, charts and blackboards are in short supply (Caillods and Postlethwaite, 1995). According to recent UN International Institute for Educational Planning (IIEP) survey studies, in the Kilosa district of Tanzania 'pupils had no textbooks at all in 52 per cent of the schools and there was an insufficiency in 79 per cent of them' (Caillods and Postlethwaite, 1995: 6). Because of high levels of poverty, 'primary school enrolment dropped in absolute terms' (Stewart, 1994: 147) in Tanzania during the 1980s.

Throughout the developing world, countries have continued to experience social, economic and political difficulties. These include a decrease in gross national productivity levels, balance of trade deficits, reduced exports and, subsequently, many developing countries have become more dependent on external donor-aid. Chahoud, (1991: 34) outlines the social effects of the SAP thus:

> For the majority of the population the so-called elimination of inefficiency in the public sector and the introduction of market-oriented prices policies mean, invariably, mass redundancies, the withdrawal of subsidies on basic foodstuffs and public transport, and cuts in public health services and education.

Political instability fuelled by military coups, inter-ethnic violence, state corruption and autocratic governance have contributed further to a general lack of social cohesion in many of these countries.

Post-Colonial Economic and Educational 'Successes'

Whilst this is the case in many African and Latin American countries, newly industrialized countries (NICs) such as Malaysia, Indonesia, South Korea and Singapore represent a model of authoritarian development oriented towards economic growth. These countries have, at least until the recent crisis, been able to secure relative economic, political and social stability despite the different ethnic cleavages and class inequalities that exist within these societies. Sustained economic growth combined with the corporate nationalism promoted by heads of state such as Malaysia's Mahathir Mohamed, supported the hegemony of a supra-class, supra-ethnic national identity. The economic success of these countries, to a significant extent, derived from the benefit of favourable commodity prices, building a strong information technology infrastructure, and a restructured economic base.

This would seem to support our earlier argument regarding the myth of 'human capital' theory stating that education is a necessary prerequisite for economic growth. In practice, there is very little concrete evidence to support the taken-for-granted correlation between education and economic development. In this instance, economic success *contributed* to an expanding higher education system. This argument is supported also in the example of the transition towards universal education in England during the First Industrial Revolution at the end of the nineteenth century. During this time, rapid economic growth facilitated by technological development and export markets ensured by the colonies provided the possibility for the growth of mass schooling. Social change typified by the development of corporate commercial organizations and the re-definition of work practices in consequence to industrialization, contributed further to the overall development of education in England during the late nineteenth century.

In light of the current economic and political crisis in South Asia, the situation is unclear. We can nevertheless argue that the contrast between the relative success of the 'tiger' economies and Sub-Saharan Africa and Latin America, serve to highlight that *policies that work in some societies, do not necessarily do so in others because of the different social and political conditions that prevail.* Such factors contradict the large scale move towards applying universal technicist approaches to social development in different parts of the world. Indeed, such interventions can be seen as forms of social engineering imposed externally on different societies through which diverse ways of life are homogenized according to standardized sets of criteria.

Structuring the New School Effectiveness Discourse

By the late 1980s many developing countries, particularly in Sub-Saharan Africa and Latin America that had been subjected to the SAP, showed poor economic outcomes including low levels of per capita income, falling investment, huge budget deficits and accelerating inflation (Stewart, 1994). These impacted negatively on the resources available for educational development and 'about half of the adjusting countries in Sub-Saharan Africa showed a decline in the education allocation ratio, with a higher proportion in Latin America (60 per cent), and a lower proportion (40 per cent) in the rest of the world' (Stewart,1994: 137). A World Bank study (1990) of 'adjusting' countries similarly found decreased performance in relation to three educational indicators including the general education allocation ratio, education expenditure per capita and gross primary school enrolment rates in comparison with other, non-adjusting, countries.

This needs to be understood in relation to the centrality within the SAP of the reallocation of resources in education which involves the introduction of 'user-charges' shifting the onus onto parents to pay for books and equipment as well as school fees. Thus whilst expenditure patterns show a steady increase in primary school funding in some adjusting countries, this needs to be balanced against decreasing levels of educational uptake in primary schools as a result of low income levels. Discussing the concept of 'people' or 'learner quality' as central to the development process, Oxenham et al. (1990: 106) state that:

> Poverty often affects the quality of learning through infrequent attendance and premature withdrawal. In India, only 25 per cent of pupils entering the first grade of primary school manage to complete the full eight-year course without repeating a year or, worse, dropping out altogether.

Within the World Bank framework, and elsewhere in educational policy contexts, emphasis has shifted from increasing levels of access to education, to concerns about quality performance in education.

A major influence on shaping the current discourse on quality in education in developing countries was the World Bank Report *Education in Sub-Saharan Africa: Policies for Adjustment, Revitalisation and Expansion* (1988). The report expressed concern about low levels of enrolment in education, erosion of quality in education including pupils' academic performance and teaching quality despite World Bank funding for educational programmes during the two preceding decades. The report advocated the adoption of three strands in educational policy.

- *Adjustment,* centred on the (1) diversification of sources of finance such as cost sharing in public education (referred to above); and (2) decreased unit costs by switching to cheaper ways of providing services and cost-effective use of resources, which included greater reliance on educational provision by non-government organizations (NGOs) and privatization.
- *Revitalization,* highlighted the need to increase the capacity of education and training systems in order to maximize quality outputs. This centred on (1) raising educational standards; (2) an efficient mix of inputs to include a minimum package of textbooks and learning materials; and (3) increased investment in the maintenance of schools' infrastructure. (World Bank, 1988).
- *Selective expansion,* concentrated on key areas such as (1) provision of universal primary education; (2) the development of distance learning programmes; (3) job-specific and occupation-specific training; (4) continuous on-the-job training; and (5) research and post-graduate education to develop human capital in order to support national scientific and technical development.

The strategies were reinforced by World Bank views on policy formulation and implementation. The 1988 World Bank report stated:

> Although the careful elaboration of educational development programs is essential, African capacity for implementation will ultimately determine the effectiveness of the programs. Improvement in education management is a necessary concomitant to policy reform and must be given immediate and continuing attention. (World Bank, 1988: 2)

Moreover, it is argued that strategic investment in education would yield broad economic benefits such as higher incomes and lower fertility to combat the steady rise in birth rate throughout the continent. Correlations thus are made between high levels of education and low birth rate, longer lifespans and better parenthood.

Of particular significance is the major role that management was to play in effecting this change, and the tying in of donor-aid with specifically targeted educational development programmes. Supported further by the discourse shaped around the need to improve the quality of education within the OECD (1989), research commissioned by the World Bank (see Lockheed and Verspoor, 1990) and UNESCO, school effectiveness has featured centrally in educational policy frameworks in developing countries. Following the *World Conference on Education for All* held in Jomtien, Thailand in 1990 (sponsored by the World Bank, UNDP, UNESCO and UNICEF) discussions on providing universal primary education have shifted to issues related to school reform, educational standards and cost-effective school management. An important theme centres on the contribution of formal education to decreasing poverty levels and maintaining sustained levels of economic growth.

World Bank discourse reaffirms human capital theory and underscores the importance of primary education in terms of securing economic growth. Thus it is argued that 'primary education is the single largest contributor to growth in both cross-country and cross-regional comparisons and the within-country analyses carried out to explain the East Asian "miracle" of development' (World Bank, 1995: 22). Stressing the complementary relationship between human and physical capital it argues further that 'a higher stock of human capital enhances the rental value of machines; and increasing stock of physical capital boosts the efficiency of educational investment; and general investment plays a weak role in economic growth when not supported by education' (World Bank, 1995: 24).

The views expressed on the East Asian miracle clearly ignore the long-term nature of evaluating educational progress. They also ignore the argument that we made above that educational development throughout this region, to a significant extent, *benefited* from a period of sustained economic growth which was the outcome of a variety of factors. The re-celebration of human capital theory as the *raison d'être* of economic development thus flies against recent historical evidence to the contrary. As is discussed above, it also failed to boost economic growth in post-colonial countries during the 1960s. Increasing 'population quality' and 'advances in knowledge' through human resource development as advocated by Schultz (1979) cannot by themselves hope to succeed in societies that operate at basic subsistence levels.

In line with views expressed within the general school effectiveness paradigm, the new emphasis within the World Bank is on the measurement of educational outcomes and value added in education. This is measured in terms of 'learning gain and the increased probability of income-earning activity' (World Bank, 1995: 46). These policy directions have been reinforced by arguments in academic research that the quality of schools, including the quality of teachers, exercises a predominant influence on pupils' learning over and above broader socioeconomic factors (Heyneman, 1986; Heyneman and Loxley, 1983; Fuller, 1986). According to Heyneman and Loxley (1983: 1184) 'the poorer the nation in economic terms, the more powerful this school effect is'. Because schools are seen to make a difference to the quality of pupils' learning they, as is the case in the industrialized world, have become the focus for particular forms of development.

Summary

The World Bank, supported by academic arguments for decreased levels of educational funding by the state, advocate that the cost of schooling be transferred to parents, local communities and business interests (Harber and Davies, 1997). This would seem to fly against the realities of existing economic, political and social conditions in many developing countries, particularly those in Africa. It is unclear as to how 'more can be achieved with less public spending' in these countries, especially since the major problem following the effects of the SAP appears to relate to absolute levels of poverty for most within these societies. As we have argued, rationalist policy approaches are often socially decontextualized. As such, they do not have the flexibility to adapt to local conditions, or the discursive focus to be able to take into account the internal dynamics of development within different societies. This lends support to the argument that the range of factors contributing to poverty and under-development, and the social conditions related to economic growth within these societies have never been fully understood within the economistic paradigm which has exercised such great influence over development policies since the 1960s (Rondinelli, 1993). Two points therefore need to be made with regard to the current policy drive for school effectiveness in the developing world:

1   Linear school effectiveness taxonomies focusing on different aspects of performativity such as teaching, finance management, classroom control, leadership, resource management, etc. cannot and do not begin to address the multi-levelled problems created by the historical legacy of unequal development during the colonial period, and its consolidation within the processes of the SAP.
2   Moreover, that everyday violence in school is a reality in many countries (including developed countries), is not to be denied.

However, rather than to add these factors to the social pathology of disadvantage and endemic 'ungovernability', these negative realities need to be evaluated against the legacy of state violence against different peoples over a long period of time throughout the developing world. This is in addition to the brutalization of people through civil wars, poverty and the patrimonial culture of corruption that prevails in many developing countries. As stated earlier, the perspectives in many school effectiveness studies, in attempting to deal with 'real world' situations, and in their aim to offer 'practical' solutions, tend to have a myopic view of historical processes and their intertextual relationship with contemporary social policy and politics in developing countries.

The concept of 'quality' viewed in relation to the complex difficulties experienced by developing countries discussed throughout this chapter, needs to be re-evaluated in terms of the quality of life experiences of children and teachers within many of these countries. Generating internal organizational efficiency and functional effectiveness would seem to be less of a priority within contexts where the majority of the people cannot afford to send their children to school on a permanent basis; where vast regions within countries still lack basic educational infrastructure; where the uncertainty of refugee status still renders large numbers of people stateless; and where parents are forced to rely on child labour as a necessary means of subsistence.

Similarly, labour market arguments in support of higher levels of education as a prerequisite of economic growth in the technological global economy, have very little relevance to those whose only guaranteed access to education is confined to the primary phase. Having basic levels of literacy and numeracy do not amount to much within the restructured global economic environment and, especially, the requirement in the information age for sophisticated levels of literacy and different knowledges in order to function effectively (Rassool, 1999). How are developing countries to be enabled to participate within the information dominated social environment which now provides the substantive basis of economic growth in the modern world? Maximizing human capital to facilitate economic growth within these societies, as is suggested in World Bank discourse, and which is implicit in the general school effectiveness framework, would therefore depend on significantly more than basic education.

The issue of equity that features within the school effectiveness paradigm of the World Bank, appears to take account of gender inequalities and disparities in provision between urban and rural regions. However, it does not take account of the structured inequalities and power relations between developing countries and the industrialized world. This includes the burdens placed on the former by the SAP as well as the trade inequalities set up in the GATT agreements which regulate trade between countries. Very often these agreements subordinate national economies to the exigencies of the world economy. In effect, with regard to exports, these generally tend to operate to the advantage of politically powerful countries. Attention needs to focus more on creating the necessary social, political and economic conditions for effective education defined in terms of personal and social benefits.

The example of school effectiveness in Apartheid South Africa concretely highlights the fact that the issue of quality in education extends beyond the measurable. For whilst schools might have been technically effective and efficient within that society during that particular milieu, the concept of quality in which these notions were embedded mainly served the interests of a predatory state. Teachers were subjected to regimentation and constant regulation to ensure that they conformed to the government's preferred ways of working. School effectiveness, within this context, served a powerful means of ideological control whilst, at the same time, keeping a 'racially' divided education system in a constant state of being under-funded. It is questionable that the technical-rational solutions offered by the new school effectiveness advocates can rectify and improve the quality of education by maximizing the functional efficiency of schools within townships and shanty towns. Indeed, such arguments reduce the scale and depth of economic, political and social problems faced by this and other developing countries to the level of operational difficulties.

Thus far most of the major development experiments conducted in developing countries and, particularly, in Sub-Saharan Africa (World Bank, 1988), have failed to live up to expectations. It is time to learn about these societies beyond the rhetoric of neo-classical economic theory and to involve these countries in charting their own development, and to redefine education in terms of the specific needs of the people living within these societies. Thus it requires a model of development that has had the benefit of input from ordinary people who live within these societies, and which aims to represent a democratic societal choice. If schools as sites of cultural transmission and reproduction are integrally related with social, economic and political systems, then educational development must form part of a reforming state. Within developing countries, the notion of school effectiveness needs to be re-evaluated in terms of self-defined educational change, of improving the quality of social life, human dignity and social justice – a life without dependence.

We suggest that the fundamental shortcomings of the 'quick-fix' solutions offered by contemporary school effectiveness approaches can be understood only in relation to specific historical influences on the shaping of the social character in different societies. The universal solutions implicit in the school effectiveness paradigm with its inherent economistic orientation towards the cost-benefits of educational rates of return, lack the scope to conceptualize the full scale of the difficulties that surround schools and education in developing countries. The irrationality of historical forms of racism, and the neo-colonial superimposition of poverty through the SAP on developing countries cannot be solved by technical-rationalist solutions. Dealing with 'real world' problems as is often alluded to in school effectiveness discourse, cannot take place meaningfully outside an understanding of socio-political and economic processes and practices within particular societies, and the relationship between these and developments within the global terrain. Unless this occurs, technical solutions offered by school effectiveness frameworks and taxonomies can only tinker with the surface aspects of educational under-development in these societies.

Questions

1 What are some of the main arguments used to associate education with national development in developing countries?
2 Why do you think that school effectiveness theory might appeal to developing countries?
3 What are your views on the 'solutions' proposed by the World Bank to educational policy in developing countries?

Chapter 7

Equity and Effectiveness: the Dissonance of Difference

Displacing the Discourse

Definitions of equity in education are problematic. Social justice and equity are often conceptualized as movements, rather than goals, or desirable end states or final victories (Bauman, 1997). There is the quantitative, distributional equality and the equality associated with social relations, participation and citizenship. There is also equity according to needs or to merit (Gewirtz, Ball and Bowe, 1995). Coleman's study (1966) suggested that equality of opportunity could not be defined simply in terms of equality of *access* to resources, but should be measured in terms of *equality of outcomes* for different social and ethnic groups. Hatcher (1998b) believes that overall standards of achievement can rise while relative inequalities remain, or even widen. However, equality is also conceptualized in relation to the liberal democratic notion of the 'common good'. For example, Griffiths (1998: 302) argues that:

> social justice is a dynamic state of affairs which is good for the common interest . . . The good depends on there being a right distribution of benefits and responsibilities.

There have always been problems associated with the measurement of equality and whether inequality is normative, that is, measured against the norms and standards of the dominant group (Atkinson, 1970; Le Grand, 1991). A common criticism of the 'equality' discourse is that it has a relativity problem. Franzway et al. (1989: 96) asked 'equal with what, or whom?' Equality is now often dismissed as an over-optimistic Enlightenment project, based on a naive moral philosophy, promising liberation and freedom from oppressive power relations. Postmodernism suggests that any kind of progress against oppression is also accompanied by its own systems of power (Morley, 1997a).

However, imperfect though equity discourses are, they can provide a framework for discussion. This chapter will consider how issues of equity, social justice, entitlements and effectiveness converge or collide. Questions will be raised about the concepts of diversity and choice embedded in school reform, and whether school effectiveness and certain elements of school improvement have discursively displaced equity concerns in education. Attention will be paid to the gaps and silences in the fictional discourses of the effective school. The chapter will also critique the notion of empowerment in relation to the range of meanings attached to it and how it relates to wider social and cultural processes. It will consider whether the social structures of gender, ethnicity, sexualities, special needs and social class have been incorporated, distorted or excluded from effectiveness thinking.

In the 1970s and 1980s some concern with social disadvantage resulted in committees of inquiry into the education of particular groups such as Warnock's report on special educational needs (1978), and the Swann Committee's report on ethnic minorities (1985). It began to be acknowledged that the allocative function of education played a role in limiting and enhancing the cultural capital of different groups. Educational achievement and access to elite educational establishments have played a major part in the reproduction of class and gender privilege. How knowledge is constructed, determined and validated is also fraught with power relations. This was recognized within the broader social terrain during the 1970s and early 1980s when the social movements of feminism, anti-racism and gay liberation began to make an impact on education in the form of equal opportunities philosophies (Thomson, 1995: 283). As we indicated in Chapter 5, the ascent to power of the left in several metropolitan local authorities meant that there was an articulation, both in policy and practice, of the place education plays in the production, reproduction and transformation of the major dimensions of social inequality.

We do not wish to promote a type of golden ageism, suggesting that pre-1988 there was a universal preoccupation with social justice. It is important to recognize that equity was heavily contested, resisted and resented. Contributors to Olowe's edited collection (1990), for example, noted how there was a marked difference between espoused equity values in education and those actually in use within Inner London before the 1988 ERA. The equity in education movement was characterized by a pessimistic activism in so far as change agents were aware of the enormity of the task and yet continued to make strategic interventions in areas such as curriculum development, employment practices, teaching materials, anti-discriminatory policies, resources and interpersonal processes. However, amidst the weight of bureaucracy generated by post-1988 educational reform, with the sharp increase in procedural and task content specification, issues of equity now appear like an indulgent luxury, or ideological extravagance.

Shaw (1990: 271) observes that there has been a values drift from the equality concerns of post-war neo-Keynesian welfarism to 'hard-nosed supply-side economic doctrines . . . The idea of social justice implicit in the former model has been replaced by utilitarian social competition'. The convergence of codes, or institutional isomorphism, and the increased use of narrow concepts of performativity as the criterion for resource allocation have marginalized issues of equity and social justice.

In Britain, New Labour, with its commitment to modernization, represents an eclectic set of values. While there is a wish to retain a social democratic commitment to social justice and equity, this is placed contradictorily alongside a desire for market competitiveness as well as the need for individuals to exercise responsibility for their own education, training and welfare needs (Avis, 1998; Blair, 1995). The latter position subscribes to Hayek's (1978) argument that the concept of equity is inapplicable to the outcomes of a spontaneous process such as a free market. In education, it appears that there has been a trade-off between equity and effectiveness, with equity perceived as incompatible with efficiency in the sense of economic growth (Okun, 1975). The contradictions between the values of marketization and those of redistributive social justice are enacted materially and routinely in institutional decision making, as Deem, Brehony and Heath (1995: 26) indicate:

> The notion of social justice, one possible element of societal needs, does not fit easily with quasi market principles, and the need for governing bodies to ensure the continued financial viability of their schools may come into conflict with social justice and with the notion of providing a universal education service.

With reference to parental choice, Reay and Ball (1997) argue that the 'new market economy in education exacerbates the consequences of unequal social power rather than alleviating them'. However, references to increasing equality of educational opportunity are widespread in Labour Government documentation. In the current Labour Government's White Paper, *Excellence in Education* (1997), David Blunkett, the Secretary of State for Education asserts:

> To overcome economic and social disadvantage and to make equality of education a reality, we must strive to eliminate, and never excuse under-achievement in the most deprived parts of our country. . . . We must overcome the spiral of disadvantage, in which alienation from or failure within the education system is passed from one generation to the next. (foreword DfEE, 1997: 3)

There appears to have been a policy rediscovery of the role that contextual factors play in influencing educational performance (Gibson and Asthana, 1998). The rearticulation of terms such as 'social disadvantage' and 'under-achievement' are evocative of the language of Plowden and Coleman, once again demonstrating intertextuality. However, a key question raised by Avis (1998: 261) is whether 'New Labour, mirroring social democracy becomes the velvet glove to the iron fist of Thatcherism'. He argues that the New Labour modernization project simply offers the *illusion* of reinstituting forms of social solidarity and offering greater equity and social justice.

There has been a transference of key concepts from older discourses and these have been re-interpreted into different hegemonic projects. This exemplifies Pecheux's view (1982) that words can change meaning in discourse depending on the site of articulation.Whereas school effectiveness was originally validated by the Conservative Government as part of a value-for-money performance culture, it has been reinforced under New Labour

– now ostensibly as a means of offering educational opportunities to those caught in the 'spiral of disadvantage'. Previous discourses of effectiveness have been hijacked, with an added dimension of social justice in an attempt to regain the moral ground lost during the Thatcher and Major years. While the effectiveness of compensatory education, with its amelioration ethos or 'bandaidism', has yet to be demonstrated, ineffective and failing schools are perceived to be significantly contributing to underachievement in socially deprived regions. Hence, the introduction of up to 25 Education Action Zones – a new form of compensatory education introduced to attack the educational consequences of poverty. These are being introduced in areas 'with a mix of underperforming schools and the highest levels of disadvantage' (DfEE, 1997: 39). Gibson and Asthana (1998: 206) note that the stated aim is to 'overcome economic and social disadvantage and to make equality of opportunity a reality' (DfEE, 1997: 3), but the proposed action is based on a belief system that this will occur through the improvement of individual schools rather than through any radical overhaul of the education system.

The preoccupation with disadvantage poses representational challenges for writing about equity, in so far as there is often the risk of further pathologizing, tokenizing or homogenizing groups in educational research. Of major significance is the fact that in the current regime of performance and accountability, there is little discursive space and few linguistic tools to address equity issues. As we have already argued, key terms such as 'empowerment' and 'equity' have been appropriated and incorporated in the New Right project. Complex power differences are usually theorized through condensed signifiers, and read off from categories already constituted (Skeggs, 1997). Categories, such as 'race', gender and social class contain explanatory power in relation to the groups they represent. However, they can also be reductive and one-dimensionalizing. We wish to argue that how we are located in economic, cultural and social relations informs our access to institutionalized organizations such as schools. At the same time, however, we would argue against social determinism by suggesting that we are positioned by structures of inequality but not completely determined or programmed by them.

There are ironies involved in discussing equity and social exclusions, while potentially setting up competitive hierarchies of oppression between the different structures of inequality (Morley, 1997b). For example, there are often competing claims of communities, who, despite shared histories of discrimination, are often in danger of eclipsing each others' struggles. There are product champions for different forms of inequality who constantly remind each other of gaps and silences. This has been apparent in recent research on parental choice. While studies such as Ball (1993) have noted how the market operates as a class strategy, other writers, such as David (1997) criticize Ball for focusing on class while excluding gender when interrogating choice processes. Equally, in the 1990s, we are frequently informed that the gender gap in education has now closed (see David, 1997). For example, by 1992, 46 per cent of girls achieved 5+ GCSE (A-C), as against 37 per cent of boys. Whereas equality of opportunity is included as a factor of effectiveness in government inspections, inspection evidence suggests that only one school in five is meeting the particular needs of one or the other sex (OFSTED, 1996a: 11).

Furthermore, while some girls are now achieving better academic results than some boys at age 16, there is little evidence to indicate that this is leading to improved post-school opportunities (OFSTED, 1996a). Questions of student destinations and transition to work have no place in school effectiveness writing. Examination performances seem to have become an end in themselves, with limited attention paid to post-16 considerations, such as career planning and access to higher education.

Walkerdine (1997) challenges the observation that gender differentials in education seem to have shown a marked decline. In her analysis of the current hysteria about boys' underachievement, she draws attention to the fact that the successful girls and the failing boys are from different class constituencies. Clearly, social class, gender, 'race', sexualities and disabilities all need to be considered when focusing on equity in education. Equality of opportunity is not simply about examination results, but also about access to the labour market, self-efficacy, citizenship and lifechances. Arnot et al. (1997: 144) comment on the unresolved gender problems, as 'the hidden curriculum still appears to produce girls with low self-esteem and confidence'. As Slee (1998) hints, we may be asking the wrong outcome questions.

The Death of Class?

The cliché – the history of education is the history of class struggle – has been subjected to significant sociological analysis. For several decades, attempts have been made by educational researchers to identify exactly how social inequalities are reproduced and how access, resources and legitimation contribute to the devaluing and delegitimizing of certain groups (Barton and Walker, 1983; Bernstein, 1975; Bowles and Gintis, 1976; Halsey, Heath and Ridge, 1980; Hargreaves, 1967; Lacey, 1970). As Ball (1998: 71) indicates, 'social class was the major, almost the only dependent variable in sociological research for . . . 40 years'. Close attention has been paid to the interrelations between social structures, social mobility, and the formation and decomposition of social inequalities.

Definitions of social class are becoming increasingly problematic in the context of enhanced material consumption and apparent mobility. It is debatable whether class in general ought to be defined by exclusion and deprivation, rather than by trying to locate attributes such as occupation and education. Social class, in educational research, is often defined in terms of occupational hierarchies, social pathology or crude indicators such as take-up of free school meals, or postal codes. It is rarely examined as a system of social relationships (Hatcher, 1998a). It is noticeable that school effectiveness literature sometimes talks of social disadvantage and poverty, but not of oppression and power relations.

It would appear that there is a persistence of class differentials in educational attainment and social class inequalities in education continue to 'display marked temporal stability, extending over decades . . .' (Goldthorpe, 1996: 483). Whereas for some societies, such as Hungary and the Czech Republic, there has been some reduction in class disparities (see Shavit and Blossfeld, 1993), there is an absence of empirical evidence to suggest that there is a *generalized and sustained* reduction in class differentials in educational attainment' (Goldthorpe, 1996: 488). Mortimore and Whitty (1997: 11) point out that 'probably the single most significant factor that currently distinguishes the most academically successful schools . . . is that only a small proportion of their pupils come from disadvantaged homes'. There remains a persistent negative correlation between most measures of social disadvantage and school achievement. Britain has experienced the largest percentage increase in income inequality internationally between 1967–92 (Dennehy, Smith and Harker, 1997); yet, school effectiveness continues to be preoccupied with standards, not structures and the input/output argument.

Not only do school effectiveness discourses fail to include attention to issues of equity, they are also based on assumptions about norms that privilege the middle classes. For example, Thrupp (1998: 211) discovered in his study of socio-economically different New Zealand schools the extent to which school effectiveness, in an academic sense, not only reflects the middle-class bias of schooling in capitalist societies but also appears to rest upon the cultural resources and responses of students from middle-class families. Elliot (1996) also points out how the effective schools movement indicators have a particular ideology rooted in the grammar school tradition. As Rea and Weiner (1998: 30) argue, the material conditions needed for educational success are concealed by the liberal myth of achievement legitimated by value-addedness.

Class bias is noticeable in the way that certain schools are automatically constructed as effective, such as those in the elite private sector. However, it would appear that strategic interventions to enhance working-class participation in elite education have also failed. The Assisted Places Scheme in Great Britain was introduced by the Conservative Government in the 1970s, and was phased out by the Labour Government in 1998. The aim was to enable academically able children, particularly from the inner city areas, with limited financial means, to attend private schools. Underpinning this project was the dubious assumption that there is a causal relationship between the private education sector and academic excellence. In 1995, total public expenditure on the scheme was £104 million. However, research on this scheme indicates that very few children of working-class parents were able to benefit. Less than 10 per cent had fathers who were manual workers, compared with 50 per cent with fathers in middle-class occupations (Whitty, Power and Edwards, 1998). There were also concerns that this scheme would distort school effectiveness league tables because the scholastic quality of the private schools was enhanced at a cost to state schools, thus reinforcing the superiority of private education. Commenting on the Assisted Places Scheme, Winch (1996: 118) notes how 'public funds are employed for educational purposes, one of whose side effects is to undermine the public education system on whose success a society depends'. Under this scheme, educational salvation was perceived as an individual, rather than a collective strategy, thus reinforcing the view that education is a private, rather than a public good. Furthermore, the low number of children from working-class families did not threaten to distort the social mix of the private schools. Skeggs (1997: 1) contends that the working classes have 'consistently been classified as dangerous, polluting, threatening, revolutionary, pathological and without respect'. Walkerdine (1995: 326) also observes how 'middle-class people often only see the working class in relations of service or as frightening others in areas of town that they do not want to enter'. So, while it was acceptable for private schools to utilize public funds set aside to widen participation of particular categories, what was less appealing was the presence of actual embodied working-class children.

Equity, Choice and Empowerment

We have argued throughout this book that power is undertheorized in school effectiveness and school improvement discourses. There are references to 'powerful learning, powerful teaching and powerful schools' (Hopkins, West and Ainscow, 1996: 14), but little about how power functions both in terms of distributive justice and in social relations. There are certain ironies here. Whereas equity concerns in education appear to have been eclipsed, empowerment has become a dominant concept in the reform of the public services (Morley, 1995, 1998a). However, it is undertheorized and ill-defined. It is associated with advocacy, participation, democracy, autonomy, capacity-building and personal change in diverse areas such as literacy, urban regeneration, special needs/disability, population policies, mental health services, community care, adult education, management and organization studies, child protection, gay and lesbian rights, international development/overseas aid, social work, youth work, housing, and health. In education, empowerment has traditionally related to pedagogical processes (Morley, 1998a). Now it is more often used in relation to entitlements and empowering consumers of the educational product, or in responses to teacher resistance. As we indicated in Chapter 4, empowered teachers are those who comply with the requirements of school effectiveness. It can also be reduced to the 'giving a voice' rhetoric associated with school governance and community participation, as we suggested in Chapter 4. For example, Hopkins, West and Ainscow (1996: 2) declare their commitment to empowerment in relation to school improvement:

> The school will seek to develop structures and create conditions which encourage collaboration and lead to the **empowerment** of individuals and groups.

Social formations are frequently ignored or pathologized and power is seen as property that is readily relinquished and redistributed. It is yet another sociological concept appropriated and incorporated in New Right reform of the public services. Having lost its radical edge, empowerment remains an abstract concept, with many evangelical and redemptive pretensions. For example, Shrewsbury (1987: 8) defines empowerment in relationship to personal efficacy which would automatically lead to social change:

> To be empowered is to recognise our abilities to act to create a more humane social order. To be empowered is to be able to engage in significant learning. To be empowered is to be able to connect with others in mutually productive ways.

Robinson (1994: 7) also links inter- and intrapersonal processes with macro systems:

> Empowerment is a personal and social process, a liberatory sense of one's own strengths, competence, creativity and freedom of action; to be empowered is to feel power surging into one from other people and from inside, specifically the power to act and grow.

O'Brien and Whitmore (1989: 309) define empowerment as:

> An interactive process through which less powerful people experience personal and social change, enabling them to achieve influence over the organizations and institutions which affect their lives, and the communities in which they live.

This interpretation constructs empowerment as inherently benign, automatically translating into positive social change. As Deem (1992) states, who becomes empowered and what they do with those powers is more crucial than an abstract notion of empowerment regarded as a 'good thing' in itself.

A key question is whether empowerment is a rhetorical device to disguise systems of domination. Parents are now deemed to be empowered through school choice. As we demonstrated in Chapter 3, the Conservative Government's education reforms, expounded in the Parents' Charter (DoE, 1991, 1994) and implemented in the 1980, 1988 and 1993 Education Acts, has sought to increase competition between schools by enhancing parental choice. Recent research studies have highlighted how parental choice, rather than contributing to the raising of standards, has reinforced social inequalities (Ball, Bowe and Gewirtz, 1995; Reay and Ball, 1997; Reay, 1996). Fitz et al. (1993) found that households where the father was not in paid employment were the least likely to have gained access to a preferred school. Those who were most successful were in professional occupations. Ball (1998: 128) argues how middle-class parents have been concerned about 'maintaining social advantage in the face of national and international labour market congestion'. It would appear that those parents already with cultural capital and social and consumer power have been empowered by school choice. Class tools such as communication skills, knowledge, information, educational qualifications operate to enhance purchasing power. Education is increasingly subject to exchange value criteria. As education is being drawn into commodity form, *buying* an education becomes a substitute for *getting* an education (Kenway et al., 1993: 116). In this construction, education is not perceived as a public investment, but as a site of private consumption (Hamilton, 1998).

Studies have demonstrated that parental choice can often be based on a fear of the mixing of respectable with non-respectable classes and the breakdown of carefully constructed boundaries between the pure and the unruly. Bagley (1996) found that there was a racialized dimension to parental choice, with many white parents believing that ethnic minority children undermine educational standards and threaten the welfare of white children. In popular consciousness the multi-racial inner city school is the antithesis of the effective school. Bagley observed that gender influenced school choice too, because ten out of eleven parents citing 'race' as an issue in school selection had a daughter as the child transferring. This seemed to exemplify deeply embedded prejudices about black masculinity and its threat to white women.

In their study, Hatcher, Troyna and Gewirtz (1996: 72) discovered that racial equality has not benefited from the move to local management of schools (LMS), with various types of social microstructures serving to 'block, deflect or render invisible issues of 'race'. Schools are no longer under pressure from local authorities to develop and implement multicultural or antiracist policies. The current focus on cost effectiveness means that racial equality, as an issue, has become marginalized. Hatcher, Troyna and Gewirtz (1996) found evidence of English as a second language teaching reduced, the lack of provision of tuition in heritage languages, black pupils being down-placed in bands and racist behaviour by white pupils being left unchallenged. 'Race' and concerns of ethnic minority parents were not included in the business of school governance. They concluded that LMS serves to reinforce existing patterns of power in society. Hatcher (1998b) also notes how there was an absence of any discussion of issues of 'race' at the papers presented at the ICSEI (International Congress for School Effectiveness and Improvement) conference in January 1998 at the University of Manchester.

The emphasis in school effectiveness on public examination results as indicators of achievement and the introduction of the National Curriculum has meant that antiracist and multicultural education have been deprioritized. As we stated in Chapter 1, this has enabled attitudes and prejudices to go unchallenged. A much publicized case of the racialized dimension of parental choice occurred in Cleveland in 1987 (Regina v Cleveland County Council). A white parent requested that her child should be transferred from a school with a large proportion of Asian children to one which was predominantly white. The Local Education Authority agreed and was challenged by the Commission for Racial Equality under the 1976 Race Relations Act. In 1991, the High Court ruled that the LEA had been legally correct in acceding to the parental request under the 1980 Education Act. In other words, education reform overrode anti-discriminatory legislation, and racially prejudiced parents were empowered.

Parental choice can also influence pedagogic styles and the micro-processes of the classroom. The persistent correlation between measured attainment and social class can suggest to schools that they should adopt strategies to attract more middle-class pupils. Boaler (1997) observed that the middle-class parents many schools aim to attract often opt for schools with streaming and setting. Connections between setting, streaming and high achievement are not necessarily substantiated by research evidence. Slavin (1996) states that:

> study after study, including randomized experiments of a quality seldom seen in educational research, finds no positive effect of ability grouping in any subject or at any grade level, even for the high achievers most widely assumed to benefit from grouping. (p. 279)

However, the grouping of children according to their ability has long been thought to *disadvantage* working class and ethnic minority children whose ability is often underestimated (Gillborn, 1997; Hargreaves, 1967; Lacey, 1970; Tomlinson, 1987). The French sociologist, Bourdieu also believed that there is an almost perfect homology between the class position of the individual pupils and their teachers' intellectual judgements of them (cited in Moi, 1991: 1024). We argue that educational ability can be socially constructed and achievement and effectiveness can be manipulated politically (see Brown, 1998).

Boaler (1997) discovered that students who learned mathematics in an open approach in mixed ability classes achieved more high grades than equivalent ability children placed in setted classes. She also found that social class had influenced setting decisions, resulting in disproportionate numbers of working-class students being allocated to low sets. One consequence of this process is that working-class children can be discursively constructed as liabilities in the race to enhance league table scores. Reay and Ball (1997: 91) discuss how the recruitment of 'desirable' students is deeply sedimented in school discourses:

> . . . within a prevailing educational culture in which school governing bodies talk openly about potential A grade pupils being more valuable than potential Ds . . . it is only a small step to begin to identify being working-class with having low social status.

The set or stream a young person is placed in, at an early age, will most certainly dictate the opportunities they receive later in their lives, as it can fix their potential achievement. This is particularly true of maths and English which act as filters for opportunities in higher education and employment. However, in spite of the potential for discriminatory and deterministic practices, setting and streaming have been bolstered by New Labour as part of their drive to increase school effectiveness (Blair, 1996). The question is who is being empowered through the school effectiveness movement and for what end?

Mapping the Universal

As we demonstrated in Chapter 6, the school effectiveness movement has flourished on an international scale, with an increasing desire to identify tangible characteristics of the effective school. Pam Sammons et al. (1995) examined school effectiveness research in a range of countries including Australia, Britain, North America and the Netherlands. They compiled a taxonomy comprising 11 characteristics:

Professional leadership	Firm and purposeful
	A participative approach
	The leading professional
Shared vision and goals	Unity of purpose
	Consistency of practice
	Collegiality and collaboration
A learning environment	An orderly atmosphere
	An attractive working environment
Concentration on teaching and learning	Maximization of learning time
	Academic emphasis
	Focus on achievement
Purposeful teaching	Efficient organization
	Clarity of purpose
	Structured lessons
	Adaptive practice
High expectations	High expectations all round
	Communicating expectations
	Providing intellectual challenge
Positive reinforcement	Clear and fair discipline
	Feedback
Monitoring progress	Monitoring pupil performance
	Evaluating school performance
Pupil rights and responsibilities	Raising pupil self-esteem
	Positions of responsibility
	Control of work
Home/school partnership	Parental involvement in their children's learning
A learning organization	School-based staff development

(Sammons et al. for OFSTED, 1995)

A noticeable feature of such taxonomies is their sense of almost algorithmic certainty and their social and political decontextualization. While there may be a correlation between particular features of schools and their degree of success, it is a major conceptual leap to suggest a causal relationship. Educational success and failure are discursively constructed, but power is an absent presence in the search for prototypes. Texts, such as taxonomies, are always produced with interests in mind. As such, they encapsulate a series of 'truths'. While appearing neutral, the indicators in school effectiveness taxonomies represent a system of governmentability. They are constructed focused forms of the regulatory gaze. Said (1984) contends that the relations of power and authority are what makes the production of texts possible. The certainty of such taxonomies denies any consideration of alternatives. There is also an assumption that so-called 'causal' factors are:

> . . . independent, universal and additive; that is, they do not interfere with each other and are uninfluenced by contexts. (Hamilton, 1998: 15)

This atomistic view of school effectiveness reflects the tradition of abstracted empiricism (Lauder, Jamieson and Wikeley, 1998). That is to say, it suggests that stable school structures and practices can be engineered and sustained.

As we have already noted, school effectiveness is based on the notion of a universal subject. Students, teachers and headteachers are a homogenized ungendered, non-racialized or social classed group. They are disembodied players in a larger project. This reflects a potent criticism of effectiveness discourses. The New Right restorational agenda sees the cognitive package as the central educational outcome. The 'child' has become an undifferentiated cognitive unit, and the teacher a disembodied intermediary. Equity has only been addressed in functionalist terms. In some cases, equity in Britain – often in the form of equal opportunities policies – is just another variable to be inserted and incorporated into OFSTED inspection checklists.

It has been left largely to feminist and anti-racist scholars such as Epstein (1993), Gillborn (1990), Griffiths and Troyna (1995), Spender (1982) and Weiner (1994), to demonstrate how schools actively construct and reproduce gender, social class, compulsory heterosexuality and racialized inequalities via the curriculum, pedagogy, organizational cultures, employment patterns and the hidden curriculum. Angus (1993: 341) argues how, in the simplistic input/output model of school effectiveness:

> Family background, social class, any notion of context, are typically re-garded as 'noise' – as outside background factors which must be controlled for and then stripped away so that the researcher can concentrate on the important domain of school factors . . . sexism, racism, and any other social and educational disadvantages and conflicts that surround and pervade schooling . . . may be remotely acknowledged, but they are sanitised in school effectiveness research, reduced to distant 'home background' and regarded merely as quality of input.

While the taxonomies of effectiveness outline school interventions for change, there is no acknowledgment of the need for wider social policies to eliminate poverty, racism, heterosexism and sexism. Change processes themselves are gendered, racialized and embedded in class relations. Foucault believed that schools, like other modern institutions, are 'factories of order', factories of predictable, and therefore controllable, situations (Foucault, cited in Bauman, 1997: 129). In taxonomies of effectiveness, the organizational world is presented as an orderly, rational surface, untainted by the mess and chaos of unequal power relations in which the lived world is constituted.

Progress, Achievement and Identity

Structures of inequality can be reproduced in the micropolitics of power in schools. Quotidian practices, processes and interactions can contribute to social inclusions, exclusions and effectiveness. It appears that to describe an overall school as effective or ineffective is misleading. Some schools are differentially effective for different social, gender and racial groups. The success of high achieving pupils can sometimes be obtained at the expense of less able peers. Equally, achievement and progress are different. Progress refers to changes in pupils' performance between two time points, rather than endpoint examination results. The progress that pupils make during schooling is described as 'value added' – a term derived from economics. This means taking account of starting points to see how much impact the school makes. Judgements about 'effective' schools are made by comparing a school's predicted performance (based on the composition of its pupil population) and its actual performance. Both Mortimore et al. (1988) and Tizzard et al. (1988) found that while attainment was influenced by the home background, progress was more likely to be influenced by schooling.

Multi-level modelling, a statistical technique, attempts to control for the various differences that might influence a pupil's performance. This technique compares the performance of similar pupils in different schools – producing a measure of the relative 'effectiveness' of individual schools. A criticism of this approach is that by attempting to isolate separate factors, analysis loses the complexity of the interconnecting processes that might contribute to or diminish pupils' achievement. Both the school and the child are fragmented, fractured and decontextualized.

In their review of research, Gillborn and Gipps, (1996) discovered that white children make greater progress than ethnic minority pupils in primary schools and tend to leave school with the highest average achievements. While acknowledging the complexities of classifying social class, they concluded that the higher the social class, the higher the academic achievement, regardless of gender and ethnic background. They raised some key questions about whether newly introduced concepts such as school effectiveness and value added have had any wide impact on teaching and learning. For example, they note that on average, black pupils have not shared equally in the increasing rates of educational achievement and that black pupils generally may be falling further behind the average achievements of the majority of peers. Considerations of why this is the case lie outside the framework of school effectiveness taxonomies.

While many schools have a declared commitment to equality of opportunity for all, several qualitative research studies have revealed negative microprocesses that impede some young people's progress and achievement. Research in primary and junior schools has recorded an unusually high degree of conflict between white teachers and African Caribbean pupils (Wright, 1986). Nehaul (1996) also found that the majority of the black children in her case studies had negative experiences of school, arising from their ethnicity, which had the effect of depressing their achievement.

Gender, 'race' and social class play important roles in the demographics of school exclusions. African Caribbean pupils are between three and six times more likely to be excluded than whites of the same sex. The OFSTED report on disaffected pupils (1993) records how young black people in one local education authority accounted for 1:4 exclusions although they made up only 1:14 pupil population. This disproportionate representation was evident in several locations, with black young people in Birmingham accounting for 32 per cent of all exclusions, while only constituting 8 per cent of the school population. Twelve and a half per cent of overall excluded pupils in a 1990 survey also had statements of special educational needs. Boys are four times as likely to be excluded from school as girls (OFSTED, 1996a).

The government report into exclusions also found an association between rates of exclusion and the proportion of pupils taking free school meals (OFSTED, 1996b). They also noted that the majority of African Caribbean children who had been excluded were of average or above average ability, but had been assessed by the schools as under-achieving. When commenting on the alarming increase in exclusions, the National Union of Teachers survey (1992) cited the increased competition between schools and the pressure from school testing and league tables as contributory factors.

It might also be that norms of behaviour are being prescribed in relation to the fictional construction of the ideal learner. The effective school is behaviourist, in that it demands particular demonstrations of educational engagement. For example, Reynolds (1991) suggests that social outcome measures are also important in school effectiveness research. However, these tend to relate to attendance, behaviour and pupils' attitudes towards school. Students are being judged according to the extent they conform and embody norms demanded by school effectiveness discourses. Any transgression leads to heavy sanctions. Emotional and social problems which might contribute to disaffected behaviour cannot be easily accommodated in the urgency to achieve good examination results. High risk students must be driven out of mainstream educational provision to protect the school's place in published league tables (Slee and Weiner, 1998). School exclusions represent the underbelly of school effectiveness. In the discourse of organizational purity and supremacy, the shadow material has to be denied and non-conformists banished.

Black and/or ethnic minority students occupy a problematic location in school effectiveness. A finding in Gillborn and Gipps' study (1996) was the extent to which South Asian pupils are sometimes subject to negative stereotypes and the remediation ethos. Language problems can be misinterpreted as learning difficulties, and Asian pupils can be inappropriately placed in lower streams and sets (Troyna and Siraj-Blatchford, 1993). One of the science teachers in Gewirtz's research exemplified this approach:

> I know that there are some students that I teach in year 11 who are not going to get graded . . . It's not because they don't come to school, it's just because their language isn't up to it at present. (Jack Taylor, cited in Gewirtz, 1997: 18)

Special needs are problematically positioned in relation to the norms and values of school effectiveness. In the current market-led culture, an effective school appears to be one which does not have too many departures from educational norms. As Gewirtz, Ball and Bowe (1995: 185/6) suggest:

> Filling up a school with 'able' children and keeping children with SEN to a minimum is the cheapest and most labour efficient way of enhancing league-table performance.

Slee (1998: 101) argues that, in spite of claims by Ramasut and Reynolds (1993: 236) that the 'school improvement movement is likely to improve the performance of children with special needs', disabled students introduce a level of diversity and educational instability which threaten the homogeneity of the effective school. As such, they become liabilities, or further chaos to be regulated, in the race for performance-oriented league tables. Thus, discriminatory educational practices may have been sanctioned in the name of school effectiveness.

Teachers are involved in the daily work of identity formation. While identity is not fixed, early years' messages about one's abilities and worth are potent contributors to self-image. In school effectiveness literature, the politics of identity of teachers and learners is overlooked. The emphasis is on the effectiveness of the school rather than on the self-efficacy of pupils. The pupil's inner world is not always considered. However, schools are social institutions in which structures of inequality can be both challenged and reproduced. By representing pupils as cognitive entities, issues relating to sexualities, gender, 'race' and coercive power relations are excluded. Affective factors such as interpersonal processes, self-esteem, confidence and a positive sense of self-worth are notoriously difficult to measure. While literacy and numeracy are of central importance as indicators of school effectiveness, little attention is paid to the part that anxiety, alienation, fear and low self-esteem play in cognitive development.

In her psychoanalytical study of teaching and learning, Shaw (1995) argues that academic subjects are containers of feelings. The gendered organization of emotional life significantly influences subject choices and preferred styles of learning. The latter has been theorized in relation to feminist pedagogy (Morley, 1998a; Weiler, 1988). Yet gender in the 1990s has been reduced to the moral panic over boys' alleged underachievement. While the 1990s have witnessed an enormous expansion of research interest in masculinities and education (see Skelton, 1998), concern over homophobia and heterosexism in schools has diminished. Epstein and Johnson (1994: 198) discuss how heterosexism:

> operates through silences and absences as well as through verbal and physical abuse or through overt discrimination. Indeed, one form of heterosexism discriminates by failing to recognise differences. It posits a totally and unambiguously heterosexual world in much the same way as certain forms of racism posit the universality of whiteness.

The social and sexual identities of pupils are not factors in school effectiveness. Yet, ironically, Stoll and Fink (1996: 129) point out that:

> . . . there is a direct connection between how pupils feel about themselves and their achievement in school.

The silencing of the challenges to compulsory heterosexuality are not seen as relevant to academic performance. Young lesbian and gay students are expected to function at their full potential, while significant aspects of their subjectivity and identity formation are denied (Epstein and Johnson, 1998). Education is often perceived as preparation for citizenship, and yet, as Richardson (1998: 88) denotes, lesbians and gay men are only partial citizens within the traditional and dominant model of citizenship. Epstein and Johnson (1994: 216) note the irony that while schools appear to offer opportunities for identity formation, sexuality is a silent discourse.

> Paradoxically, sexual constructions are all-pervasive in the school context, while, at the same time, sexuality is specifically and vehemently excluded from the formal curriculum or confined to very specific and heavily guarded spaces. (Epstein and Johnson, 1994: 216)

We note the irony too, that even in excellent collections deconstructing the power base of school effectiveness such as Slee, Weiner and Tomlinson (1998), no mention is made of sexualities in the many discussions of equity. It would seem that the gaps and silences in education reform and even in the work of its most articulate critics, have reinstitutionalized hegemonic forms of heterosexuality. There are dangers of objectification and a production-line approach to education that excludes vast areas of young people's social, emotional, cultural, psychological and political experiences.

Summary

In this chapter, we have argued that:

- school effectiveness is a normalizing discourse, culturally and psychically reinforced;
- the notion of a universal subject positions special needs, gays and lesbians, ethnic minorities, the working classes as stigmatized 'other' in pervasive organizational cultures;
- curriculum fundamentalism has excluded consideration of the social dimension of education;
- the momentum of the market places the responsibility for success or failure on the individual child, parent or school;
- there are major gaps and silences in school effectiveness theory relating to identity, culture and difference;
- school effectiveness writing is not embedded in sociological concepts. Some contextual rhetoric is sometimes tokenistically alluded to and then disregarded;
- there has been a transition from the social to the cognitive and from the notion of education as a public good to the atomized view that it is a private good.

Smith and Noble (1995: 21) indicate that:

> The massive differences between different social groups remain, but they can now be individualised out of sight.

Bourdieu claimed that the educational system is one of the principal agents of symbolic violence in modern democracies. It legitimates dominant power structures and attempts to make us believe that the powerful are fit to rule us by virtue of their qualifications, rather than by virtue of their class privilege (cited in Moi, 1991). A central aspect of hegemony is that power relations become so naturalized that they remain unquestioned. As we argued in Chapter 6, the school effectiveness discourse lacks a view of history, and of people in the complexity of their lives. It presents itself as non-ideological whilst it rationalizes a view of the world in which control is all-encompassing. We argue that the exclusion of socio-economic factors and the lack of attention to equity issues in school effectiveness reinforce traditional power relations, and function as disciplinary and regulatory mechanisms for ensuring conformity.

Questions

1 What role, if any, do you believe that education plays in:
   i. challenging social disadvantage?
   ii. reproducing social disadvantage?
2 What is your understanding of the concept of empowerment?
3 What, in your view, are the positive and negative aspects of parental choice?
4 Could you construct a checklist for school effectiveness that incorporates issues of equity, social justice, identities and culture?

Chapter 8

Conclusion: Redefining Change

School effectiveness has become a vast industry, legitimized through public policy, finance and educational research. As a relay of power, it currently frames the language of school practice and management. We have attempted to fracture the discourse by uncovering its epistemological bases. We have aimed to open up some discursive space, as a counterpart to the closure and certainty embedded in school effectiveness. It has been an objective to uncover submerged structures and ideologies, as well as mechanisms to ensure reproduction and transformation. We have endeavoured to interrogate what is hidden, contradictory, silenced, distorted and avoided in the common-sense rhetoric, and to show how regimes of truth coagulate politically and historically. Thus, we have identified the significance of intertextuality in shaping educational debate.

School effectiveness is not new. It has been captured from a variety of ideological milieux and reinterpreted and given new meanings within the ideological framework of the free market. We have raised questions about the validity of applying the concept of the free market, with its rationalist logic, to education. Education is discursive, with diverse sets of aims that extend beyond the measurable. It does not only revolve around examination results. It deals with the development of diverse groups of people in relation to culture and society. The depiction of teachers in 'failing' schools as 'sinners' or deviants from constructed norms detracts from their role as cultural workers, as agents of self-definitional and cultural change.

Our exploration demonstrates how school effectiveness is a bricolage, or patchwork of different ideologies, incorporating systems theory, human capital theory, regulation theory, new managerialism and Japanese work practices and concepts of organizational development such as *kaizen* and *kaisha*. As an eclectic pastiche inserted into a rigid modernist framework, school effectiveness abounds with normative procedures and performance management. With its commitment to creating a common value system, school effectiveness could be seen to represent an insidious form of Japanization of the education system, suggesting a particular production line and corporate model of success. The emphasis on measurable output quality, taxonomies and target setting have created the totalization of control, resulting in organizational isomorphism and self-regulating mechanisms for educational change. In Britain, educational reform under the Conservative Government, was based on quasi-market competitive pressures. Under the present Labour government, the pressure is applied through performance targets and an ostensible commitment to excellence. This particular notion of excellence is linked to the elitism grounded in the grammar school system. Even though New Labour has reinserted the concept of disadvantage via Education Action Zones, both models assume that schools can perform independently of contextual constraints. Both New Labour and the Conservatives also share a belief that educational policy should be influenced by global competition and the need to reconstruct the welfare state in conformity with it (DfEE, 1997; Hatcher, 1998b).

Although school effectiveness represents an eclectic mix of theories, we have argued that new managerialism is a dominant thread. This emphasizes managing the crises within schools, chaos, finance and human resources. Everything can be regulated by the market and management rationalities. It involves new structures, and new regimes of regulation, introduced largely from the corporate context of the private sector. School effectiveness combines culture management (the creation of purposes and meanings) with performance management (measuring what really matters). The introduction of markets and managers has been a generic transformational device designed to restructure and reorient public service provision. The performance ethos has created an audit explosion, with a proliferation of evaluative procedures. School effectiveness has constructed new institutional norms and patterns, and new logics of appropriateness. There have been structural realignments between purchasers and providers. There has also been an incorporation and appropriation of radical language associated with community and consumer rights. The consumer has replaced the citizen, with the accompanying rhetoric of empowerment, community participation and choice.

We have argued that school effectiveness is dominated by a logic of causality and lacks a coherent analysis of power. There are many questions about interpretation and causality in effectiveness research. For example, Pennycuick, (1993) reports that establishing a statistically significant correlation between two variables, such as class size and test results, does not automatically establish causality. Effectiveness has been reduced largely to those schools which perform well in examinations, as Rose (1995: 3) indicates:

> If we determine success primarily in terms of test scores, then we ignore the social, moral and aesthetic dimensions of teaching and learning – and, as well, we'll miss those considerable intellectual achievements which aren't easily quantifiable.

Whereas equity measures in the 1980s were perceived as the politicization of education, school effectiveness is presented as a neutral scientistic discourse. It offers tangible change and engages with 'real world' classroom issues. Rather than being rational/neutral, it is deeply enmeshed with the ideology of the market which excludes social factors. By failing to challenge oppressive cultural meanings attached to special needs, social class, gender, 'race' and sexualities, it is deeply political. There has been an onslaught on diversity in the name of rationality, economy and efficiency. Effectiveness and excellence have displaced equity and there appears to have been an erosion of collective memory of counter-hegemonic interventions from the 1970s and 1980s. We support a broader definition of school performance that considers the social, emotional and political contexts of teaching and learning.

Using a form of policy archaeology, we have outlined the development of the moral panic over standards and its policy solutions. We have traced the contours of the ideological break with welfare interventionism, showing how the perceived decline in educational standards in state education and, especially within the comprehensive school system, was placed in stark juxtaposition with earlier possibilities of excellence offered in the selective grammar school system. Drawing on influential research studies, government reports and policy documents, we have demonstrated how concerns with national prosperity, equality of opportunity and the needs of capital have waxed and waned in their influences on theories of educational change. One binary that is repeatedly left unresolved is the home or school dilemma. Recent school effectiveness findings still point to schools having an independent effect of only 8–15 per cent on student outcomes (see Hatcher et al., 1996). We argue for a nuanced attention to both, in so far as any technology for change needs to be socially contextualized. We would also call for a deconstruction of the social, with an understanding of how structures of inequality inter-relate. In relation to educational development in an international context, attention also needs to be paid to cultural transfer and whether a universal theory of effectiveness can exist, or whether, indeed, it represents a continuation of neo-colonial hegemonies.

Policy documents and influential studies often frame effectiveness in terms of formal and informal binaries. The effectiveness discourse itself is perceived as the universal panacea for educational ills by its advocates, or dismissed as too technicist and positivistic by its critics (Morley, 1998b). Multi-dimensional concepts, such as quality, are often reduced to binaries. Quality is a subjective category of description and its meaning derives from its point of articulation. Hoppers (1994: 175) reminds us that:

> Quality is a multi-dimensional concept and its interpretation is dependent on the interests of the different actors in the process and outcomes in the enterprise.

Ball (1997) argues that quality, within the school effectiveness discourse, is a technology for cultural engineering, with strong normative connotations. He believes that quality is 'a "relay device" effectively linking government "mentalities" and policies, with everyday organisational realities' (p. 327). In this analysis, 'good' schools are those which display a commitment to performing policy priorities. We argue that the preoccupation with performance is having a detrimental effect on more complex areas of school life, such as the affective and aesthetic domains. Schools have been reinvented as financial bodies, and, as we argued in Chapter 3, a new audit culture has emerged. The common elements of school effectiveness have involved site-based management, the language of improvement and budgetary devolution. Funding regimes have become structuring mechanisms. Organizational culture is presented as monolithic, unified and consensual. However, we live in a complex world, in which certainties about sexualities, social class, nationalities and abilities exist in a constant state of flux. With school effectiveness there is an assumption that fixed variables and effects are identifiable and reproducible. Effectiveness is defined as a set of organizational change techniques which can be harnessed to any chosen educational objectives (Hatcher, 1998b: 275). We strongly challenge modernist assumptions of the universal subject i.e. once a set of truths are established, they hold good for all schools, teachers, children, parents within all contexts.

We believe that school effectiveness, while appearing to be a rational, algorithmic, modernist formula for educational change, is riven with contradictions. While dealing with absolutes in the form of attainable standards, and universalizing subjects, it also encapsulates some of postmodernist thinking on the regulatory force of capillary power. That is that power is everywhere in the microprocesses of everyday life and that people internalize dominant values and learn to regulate themselves. Similarly, whilst school effectiveness appears to embrace the boundary-crossing and flexibility of post-Fordism, in practice, it incorporates neo-Taylorist rigidities. However, we recognize that, in times of significant social upheaval, a major appeal of school effectiveness is its certainty and the alleged connections between input and output. It has offered some exactitudes to teachers, parents, children and policy-makers. There is invariably some correspondence between social structures and mental structures. With school effectiveness, everyone knows exactly where they are. Brown (1998: 33) argues that:

> The publication of league tables in relation to examination results . . . can improve the effectiveness of an individual school, by stimulating a useful process of analysis and action which leads to a genuine raising of standards.

This summative evaluation of schools' performance can be a useful tool to generate debate. Interpretation depends on assumptions about what constitutes normal and average achievement. For example, in a multi-cultural, heterogeneous society such as Britain, what constitutes average achievement? We acknowledge that this observation could be said to be taking us down the path of global relativism, suggesting that there is no fixed point from which to speak. However, a challenge remains as to whether judgements about effective or ineffective schooling or education can be made without resorting to homogenizing distortions and bounded discourses. Hatcher (1998b: 268) reminds us that there is a crucial distinction between absolute and relative levels of attainment. A question is whether effective schools, as defined by the school effectiveness movement, actually exist, and whether the characteristics are transferable from one location to another. In other words, are effective schools simply identified, or can they be actively constructed and reproduced?

School effectiveness represents a marketable prescription for educational change. The internationalization of market forces now underpins educational policy. We have both worked in 'developing' countries where the certainty of school effectiveness has provided a welcome structure in the midst of educational problems on an overwhelming scale, such as in India. Equally, in post-apartheid South Africa, where there is so much need for redress after decades of repression, the clarity of school effectiveness has some appeal. However, it could be argued, within that context, that the effective school is constructed on the lines of white minority educational provision, with black schools appearing more effective, the more they conform to norms dictated by the dominant group. Within the international context, school effectiveness represents a form of order to donor organizations. In the face of intractable problems such as poverty, child labour, low school attendance and poor teacher education, school effectiveness formulae represent a starting point, a form of action. Critical appraisal of the discourse can appear as Western self-indulgence when there is so much urgent business to address.

Whenever one attempts to deconstruct regimes of truth embedded in change theories, there is always the risk of leaving readers stripped of any form of certainties and fearful of any type of action. The large investors, such as aid organizations and national and local governments, want 'objective' indicators of what their investment yields. However, there are dangers of replicating colonial hegemonies, with a more sophisticated rendition of the 'we know what is best for you' rhetoric of educational development. As a form of socially decontextualized site management, school effectiveness does not address major structural inequalities. The simplistic neo-classical input-output concept of development theories erases consideration of the complexities of power differences, social diversity and historical legacies of inequality. Furthermore, the atomistic approach to school effectiveness, with the emphasis on variables and factors, can lead to charges of reductionism, with broader aims and achievements, such as values, behaviours and attitudes, more difficult to measure (Hoppers and Little, 1994). As we have indicated, non-measurable variables involved in the education process, such as the hidden curriculum and the social construction of 'race', class and gender and sexualities have been neglected. For example, Hoppers and Little (1994: 222) note the trend for complex gender inequalities in developing countries to be reduced to relative numbers of boys and girls enrolled in schools:

> To date, much gender-oriented research in primary education in developing countries has focused on questions of access and retention.

While access and retention are crucial issues, they need to be linked with broader social problems such as poverty and the effects of structural adjustment programmes. They need to be contextualized within particular societies and specific conditions that exist. In other words, these considerations are relational, rather than independent factors. Davies (1997) suggests that we also have to consider what boys and girls are gaining access to.

> Equal access to a stereotypical curriculum and equal entitlement to an equitable and hostile set of gender relations in an institution are not likely to challenge surrounding disparities in work and family, and may even compound them. (Davies, 1997: 88)

In Britain, gender issues in education have been reduced to examination performance. The subtleties of the micropolitics of gendered and racialized processes are lost in school effectiveness.

The manufactured crisis has produced a kind of war effort in education. Teachers have been constructed as change agents, as 'key actors in the production of a better education system' (Riddell and Brown, 1991: 2). After having been cast as 'passive observers in an unalterable process' (Riddell and Brown, 1991: 2), teachers are now reassured that their interventions make a difference. They have targets, goals, visible indices of their efforts. There is a new classification and value creation machinery, based on a moral authority, backed up with quantification and a series of sign systems which represent educational excellence.

However, while there is a powerful rhetoric of empowerment, teachers have been moved away from their role as cultural workers and repositioned as functionaries and technicians. This is underpinned by a potent emotional subtext, with blame, shame and responsibility externalized and projected on to individual schools and teachers. In many cases, the only form of resistance left to teachers is stress and exit from the profession. In addition to the enhanced bureaucratic procedures, the rhetoric of improvement starts with guilt, lack, deficit, public shaming – a type of educational *mea culpa*, with failing schools representing a form of damnation. The setting up of Education Action Zones shares similarities with the continuous improvement principles of *kaizen* and Total Quality Management. The difference is that here it takes place not only within the micro-context of individual school process but also under the omnipotent and omniscient gaze of centralized, national technologies of control. Schools are kept under constant surveillance, with the OFSTED inspection process serving to consolidate a technocratic power base. Checklists and taxonomies are focused forms of the gaze. There is a constant struggle for perfection with OFSTED inspections representing an educational equivalent to the 'zero-defect' guarantee from Total Quality Control practices in industry.

We are not arguing for inactivity, lack of accountability nor that schools do not need to change. But, rather than focusing on a series of binaries, we would argue for subtle attention to social, organizational, pedagogical and political contexts of educational change and development. Ideas about educational change have been reworked and rearticulated in a new configuration of power. We maintain that knowledge and academic achievement are not neutral. They are culturally defined, determined and constructed. The ubiquitous use of terms such as 'effectiveness', 'quality' and 'achievement' does not automatically denote shared meanings and common understandings. It could be argued that achievement is almost entirely dependent on socially defined structures and opportunities. School effectiveness is part of the modernization paradigm which associates the development of skills with enhanced productivity. As New Labour has indicated in their White Paper (DfEE, 1997), an aspect of the rationale for school effectiveness has been the need for enhancing national productivity and international competitiveness. The segmentation of the educational market and the creation of competition between schools has simply led to uneven, individualized solutions. The market is inelastic and schools can only poach from each other. Resources are simply moved around, so that the league table of one school may rise, without necessarily having any impact on national productivity.

Effectiveness discourses have become new master narratives in education. The school effectiveness movement, and now its operational arm – school improvement – are utilitarian solutions to a largely manufactured crisis over standards. The gaps and silences are also politically significant. School effectiveness raises questions about what works, rather than about whose interests are being served. Opportunities to debate the issue of competing interests and perceptions are limited. School effectiveness and school improvement are powerful policy condensates, demanding consensus and orthodoxy. They exemplify the steering at a distance trend in public policy whereby education is more overtly tied in to national economic interests while giving the appearance of site-based autonomy (Ball, 1998). School effectiveness policy and discourse screen out alternative realities and possibilities for action. It is questionable, in such a diverse and rapidly changing social world, whether absolute standards can ever exist. As we have indicated, concepts such as quality, improvement, management and effectiveness are not value-free and indeed, are saturated with power relations.

References

ADLER, M., PETCH, A., and TWEEDIE, J. (1989) *Parental Choice and Educational Policy*, Edinburgh: Edinburgh University Press.

AGLIETTA, M. (1979) *A Theory of Capitalist Regulation: The US Experience*, London and New York: Verso.

ANGUS, L. (1993) 'The sociology of school effectiveness', *British Journal of Sociology of Education*, **14**, 3, pp. 333–45.

ANGUS, L. (1994) Sociological Analysis of Educational Management, *British Journal of Sociology of Education*, **15**, 1, 79–92.

ARGYRIS, C. (1992) *On Organizational Learning*, Oxford: Basil Blackwell Publishers Ltd.

ARGYRIS, C., and SCHON, D.A. (1996) *Organizational Learning II: Theory, Method and Practice*, Reading, MA: Addison-Wesley Publishing Company.

ARNOT, M., DAVID, M., and WEINER, G. (1997) 'Educational reform, gender equality and school cultures', in COSIN, B., and HALES, M. (eds) *Families, Education and Social Differences*, London: Open University/Routledge, pp. 132–48.

ASPINALL, K., and PEDLER, M. (1996) 'Schools as learning organisations', in FIDLER, B., RUSSELL, S., and SIMKINS, T. (eds) *Choices for Self-Managing Schools: Autonomy and Accountability*, London: Paul Chapman Publishing Ltd, pp. 227–42.

ATKINSON, A.B. (1970) 'On the measurement of inequality', *Journal of Economic Theory*, **2**, 3, 244–63.

AVIS, J. (1998) '(Im)possible dream: post-Fordism, stakeholding and post-compulsory education', *Journal of Education Policy*, **13**, 2, 251–63.

AVIS, J., BLOOMER, M., ESLAND, G., GLEESON, D., and HODKINSON, P. (1996) *Knowledge and Nationhood: Education, Politics and Work*, London: Cassell.

BACCHUS, M.K. (1997) 'Education for development and social justice in the Third World', in SCRASE, T.J. (ed.) *Social Justice and Third World Education*, New York and London: Garland Publishing Inc., pp. 3–32.

BAGLEY, C. (1996) 'Black and white unite or flight? The racialised dimension of schooling and parental choice', *British Educational Research Journal*, **22**, 5, 569–80.

BALL, S.J. (1981) *Beachside Comprehensive: a Case-Study of Secondary Schooling*, Cambridge: Cambridge University Press.

BALL, S.J. (1983) 'Imperialism, social control and the colonial curriculum in Africa', *Journal of Curriculum Studies*, **15**, 3, 237–63.

BALL, S.J. (1987) *The Micropolitics of the School*, London: Routledge.

BALL, S.J. (1990) *Politics and Policy Making in Education: Explorations in Policy Sociology*, London: Routledge.

BALL, S.J. (1990) 'Management as moral technology: A Luddite analysis', in BALL, S.J. (ed.), *Foucault and Education*, London: Routledge, pp. 153–66.

BALL, S.J. (1993) 'Education markets, choice and social class', *British Journal of Sociology of Education*, **14**, 3–19.

BALL, S.J. (1993) 'Education policy, power relations and teacher's work', *British Journal of Educational Studies*, **41**, 2, 106–21.

BALL, S.J. (1994) *Education Reform: a Critical and Post-Structuralist Approach*, Milton Keynes: Open University.

BALL, S.J. (1995) 'Intellectuals or technicians? The urgent role of theory in educational studies', *British Journal of Educational Studies*, **XXXX111**, 3, 255–71.

BALL, S.J. (1997) 'Good school/bad school: paradox and fabrication', *British Journal of Sociology of Education*, **18**, 3, 317–36.

BALL, S.J. (1998) 'Big policies/small world: an introduction to international perspectives in education policy, *Comparative Education*, **34**, 2, 119–30.

BALL, S.J. (1998) 'Educational studies, policy entrepreneurship and social theory', in SLEE, R., WEINER, G., and TOMLINSON, S. (eds), *School Effectiveness for Whom? Challenges to the School Effectiveness and School Improvement Movements*, London: Falmer Press, pp. 70–83.

BALL, S.J., BOWE, R., and GEWIRTZ, S. (1995) 'Circuits of schooling: a sociological exploration of parental choice of school in social class contexts', *Sociological Review*, **43**, 52–78.

BANNO, J. (1997) *The Political Economy of Japanese Society, Volume 1, The State or the Market?*, Oxford: Oxford University Press.

BANTING, K. (1985) 'Poverty and educational priority', in McNAY, I., and OZGA, J. (eds) *Policy Making in Education*, Oxford: Pergamon Press, pp. 291–314.

BARBER, M. (1996) *The Learning Game: Arguments for a Learning Revolution*, London: Gollancz.

BARNES, D. (1969) *Language, the Learner and the School: A Research Report*, Harmondsworth: Penguin.

BARNES, D. (1976) *From Communication to Curriculum*, Harmondsworth: Penguin.

BARNES, D., and TODD, F. (1977) *Communication and Learning in Small Groups*, London: Routledge and Kegan Paul.

BARTON, L., and WALKER, S. (eds), (1983) *Race, Class and Education*. Beckenham: Croom Helm.

BAUMAN, Z. (1995) 'Searching for a centre that holds', in FEATHERSTONE, M. et al. (eds) *Global Modernities*, London: Sage.

BAUMAN, Z. (1997) *Postmodernity and Its Discontents*, Cambridge: Polity.

BECK, U. (1992) *Risk Society*, London: Sage.

BELL, L., and ARNOLD, F. (1987) 'Towards the introduction of staff appraisal into schools', *School Organisation*, **7**, 2, 193–207.

BENNETT, N. (1976) *Teaching Styles and Pupil Progress*, London: Open Books.

BERESFORD, J. (1996) 'Classroom conditions for school improvement: a literature review', occasional paper, University of Cambridge, Institute of Education.

BERNSTEIN, B. (1970) 'Education cannot compensate for society', *New Society*, **387**, 344–47.

BERNSTEIN, B. (1971) *Class, Codes and Control V1 – Theoretical Studies Towards a Sociology of Language*, London: Routledge and Kegan Paul.

BERNSTEIN, B. (1975) *On the Classification and Framing of Educational Knowledge. Class Codes and Control*, 1st edn, London: Routledge and Kegan Paul.

References

BERNSTEIN, B. (1977) *Class, Codes and Control V3 Towards a Theory of Educational Transmissions*, London: Routledge and Kegan Paul.

BHOLA, H.S. (1984) *Campaigning for literacy: eight national experiences of the twentieth century, with a memorandum to decision-makers*, Paris: UNESCO.

BLAIR, T. (1995) 'The rights we enjoy reflect the duties we owe', *The Spectator Lecture*, London, 22 March.

BLAIR, T. (1996) 'Comprehensive schools: a new vision', speech by Rt. Hon. Tony Blair, at Didcot Girls' School, Oxfordshire, Friday 7 June (Labour Party Press Release).

BOALER, J. (1997) 'Setting, social class and survival of the quickest', *British Educational Research Journal*, **23**, 5, 575–95.

BONEFELD, W. (1987) 'Reformulation of state theory', *Capital and Class*, **33**, Winter, 96–128.

BOURDIEU, P. (1977) *Reproduction in Education: Society and Culture*, London: Sage.

BOWE, R., BALL, S., and GEWIRTZ, S. (1994) 'Parental choice, consumption and social theory: the operation of micro markets in education', *British Journal of Educational Studies*, **42**, 38–53.

BOWLES, S., and GINTIS, H. (1976) *Schooling in Capitalist America*, London: Routledge and Kegan Paul.

BRATTON, J. (1992) *Japanization at Work: Managerial Studies for the 1990s*, London: Macmillan.

BRIMBLECOMBE, N. et al. (1996) 'Gender differences in teacher response to school inspection', *Educational Studies*, **22**, 1, 27–40.

BROWN, M. (1998) 'The tyranny of the international horse race', in SLEE, R., WEINER, G., and S. TOMLINSON (eds), *School Effectiveness for Whom? Challenges to the School Effectiveness and School Improvement Movements*, London: Falmer Press, pp. 33–47.

BROWN, P., and LAUDER, H. (1992) *Education for Economic Survival: From Fordism to post-Fordism?*, London: Routledge.

BUTTERFIELD, S. (1998) 'Conditions for choice? The context for implementation of curricular pathways in the curriculum', 14–19, in England and Wales. *Cambridge Journal of Education*, **28**, 1, 9–20.

CAILLODS, F. and POSTLETHWAITE, T. (1995) 'Teaching/learning conditions in developing countries', in HALLAK, J., and CAILLODS, F. (eds) *Educational Planning: The International Dimension*, UNESCO Bureau of Education; International Institute for Educational Planning, London: Garland Publishing, pp. 3–23.

CALDWELL, B., and SPINKS, J. (1988) *The Self-Managing School*, Lewes: Falmer Press.

CALDWELL, B., and SPINKS, J. (1992) *Leading the Self-Managing School*, Lewes: Falmer Press.

CALLAGHAN, J. (1976) Ruskin College Speech, 18 October 1976, from *The Times Educational Supplement*, 22 October 1979.

CCCS, 1981, *Unpopular Education: Schooling and Social Democracy in England since 1944*, London: Hutchinson in association with The Centre for Contemporary Cultural Studies, University of Birmingham.

CHAHOUD, T. (1991) 'The changing roles of the IMF and the world bank', in ALTVATER, E. et al. (eds), *The Poverty of Nations: A Guide to the Debt Crisis from Argentina to Zaire*, London: Zed Books, pp. 29–35.

CHITTY, C. (1989) *Towards a New Education System: The Victory of the New Right?* London: Falmer Press.

CHUBB, J., and MOE, T. (1992) *A Lesson in School Reform from Great Britain*, Washington: The Brookings Institute.

CLARKE, J., and NEWMAN, J. (1997) *The Managerial State*, London: Sage.

CLARKE, J., COCHRANE, A., and McLAUGHLIN, E. (1994) *Managing Social Policy*, London: Sage.

CLEGG, S. (1990) *Modern Organizations: Organization Studies in the Postmodern World*, London: Sage.

COLEMAN, J. et al., (1966) *Equality of Educational Opportunity*, Washington, DC: US Dept. of Health, Education and Welfare.

Commonwealth Secretariat, (1991) *Improving the Quality of Basic Education*, London: Commonwealth Secretariat.

COOPER, C., and KELLY., M. (1993) 'Occupational stress in head teachers: a national UK study', *British Journal of Educational Psychology*, **63**, 130–43.

Cox, C.B., and DYSON, A.E. (1975) *The Fight for Education*, Black Paper, 5, London: Dent.

Cox, C.B., and DYSON, A.E. (1975) *The Black Papers in Education*, London: The Critical Quarterly Society.

Cox, D. (1992) 'Crisis and opportunity in health service management, in LOVERIDGE, R., and STARKEY, K. (eds), *Continuity and Crisis in the NHS*, Buckingham: Open University Press.

CRAFT, M., RAYNOR, J., and COHEN, L. (eds), (1980) *Linking Home and School: a new series*, London: Harper and Row.

CREEMERS, B.P.M. (1994) 'The history, value and purpose of school effectiveness studies', in REYNOLDS, D., CREEMERS, B.P.M., NESSELRODT, P.S., STRINGFIELD, S., and TEDDLIE, C. (eds), *Advances in School Effectiveness Research and Practice*, Kidlington: Pergamon, Elsevier Science.

CROLL, P. (1986) *Systematic Classroom Observation*, London and Philadelphia: Falmer Press.

DAVID, M. (1993) *Parents, Gender and Education Reform*, Cambridge: Polity Press.

DAVID, M. (1997) 'Diversity, choice and gender', *Oxford Review of Education*, **23**, 1, 77–87.

DAVIES, L. (1990) *Equity and Efficiency? School Management in an International Context*, London: Falmer Press.

DAVIES, L. (1997) 'Education and gender relations in Africa', in SCRASE, R. (ed.), *Social Justice and Third World Education*, New York: Garland, pp. 85–105.

DAY, C. (1997) 'Teachers in the twenty-first century: time to renew the vision', in HARGREAVES, A., and EVANS, R. (eds), *Beyond Educational Reform*, Buckingham: Open University Press, pp. 44–61.

DE VROEY, M. (1984) 'A regulation approach interpretation of the contemporary crisis', *Capital and Class*, **23**, Summer, 44–5.

DEARING, R. (1997) *Higher Education in the learning society*, London: HMSO.

DEEM, R., BREHONY, K., and HEATH, S. (1995) *Active Citizenship and the Governing of Schools*, Buckingham: Open University.

DEEM, R. (1990) 'The reform of school-governing bodies: the power of the consumer over the producer?' in FLUDE, M. and HAMMER, M. (eds) *The Education Reform Act 1988: Its origins and implications*, Basingstoke: Falmer Press, pp. 153–72.

DEEM, R. (1992) 'School governing bodies – public concerns and private interests', paper presented to the International Conference on Accountability and Control in Educational Settings, CEDAR, University of Warwick.

References

DENNEHY, A., SMITH, L., HARKER, P. (1997) 'Not to be ignored: young people, poverty and health', in WALKER, C., and WALKER, A. (eds), *Britain Divided: the Growth of Social Exclusion in the 1980s and 1990s*, London: Child Poverty Action Group.

DES Circular 12/91 *Development Planning: A Practical Guide*, London: HMSO.

DES (1977a) *Education in Schools: A Consultative Paper*, Cmnd 6869, Green Paper, London: HMSO, July.

DES (1977b) *A New Partnership for Our Schools*. (The Taylor Report), London: HMSO.

DES (1985) *Better Schools*, White Paper presented to Parliament by the Secretary of State for Education and Science and the Secretary of State for Wales by Command of Her Majesty, March 1985, London: HMSO.

DES (1986) *The Effects of Local Authority Expenditure policies on Educational Provision in England 1985*, London: HMSO.

DES (1989a) *LEATGS and ESGs: National Curriculum Development Plans*, London: HMSO.

DES (1989b) *The Education (School Curriculum and Related Information) Regulations, Circular 14/89*, London: HMSO.

DES (1989c) *School Teacher Appraisal: A National Framework: Report of the National Steering Group on the School Teacher Appraisal Study*, London: HMSO.

DES (1989d) *Design and Technology in the National Curriculum*, London: HMSO.

DES (1989e) *Planning for School Development*. London: HMSO.

DES (1991) *School Teacher Appraisal: Regulations and Circular, 12/91*, London: DES.

DES (1992) *Curriculum Organisation and Classroom Practice in Primary Schools: A Discussion Paper*, London: HMSO.

DfEE (1997) *Excellence in Schools*. White Paper presented to Parliament by the Secretary of State for Education and Employment by Command of Her Majesty, July 1997, London: HMSO.

DfEE (1998) *Teachers – Meeting the Challenge of Change*, Green Paper, London: HMSO.

DiMAGGIO, P., and POWELL, W. (1983) 'The iron cage revisited: institutional isomorphism and collective rationality in organizational fields'. *American Sociological Review*, **48**, 2, 147–60.

DoE (1991) *The Parents' Charter, You and Your Child's Education*, London: HMSO.

DoE (1992) *Choice and Diversity: A New Framework for Schools*, White Paper Cm.2021. London: HMSO.

DoE (1994) *Our Children's Education: The Updated Parents' Charter*, London: HMSO.

EDMONDS, R. (1979) 'Effective schools for the urban poor'. *Educational Leadership*, October, 15–34.

EDWARDS, A.D., and FURLONG, V.J. (1978) *The Language of Teaching*, London: Heinemann.

EDWARDS, T., GERWITZ, S., and WHITTY, G. (1992) 'Researching a policy in progress: the city technology colleges initiative', *Research Papers in Education: Policy and Practice*, **7**, 1, March, 79–104.

ELLIOT, J. (1996) 'School effectiveness research and its critics: alternative visions of schooling', *Cambridge Journal of Education*, **26**, 199–223.

ELLIOTT, J. et al. (1979) 'Implementing school-based action-research: some hypotheses', *Cambridge Journal of Education*, **9**, 1, 55–71.

ELMORE, R.F., and McLAUGHLIN, M. (1988) *Steady Work: Policy, Practice and the Reform of American Education* (Report for the National Institute of Education No. R-3574-NIE/RC), The RAND Corporation.

EPSTEIN, D., and JOHNSON, R. (1994) 'On the straight and narrow: the heterosexual presumption, homophobias and schools', in EPSTEIN, D. (ed.), *Challenging Lesbian and Gay Inequalities in Education*, Buckingham: Open University Press, pp. 197–230.

EPSTEIN, D., and JOHNSON, R. (1998) *Schooling Sexualities*, Buckingham: Open University Press.

EPSTEIN, D. (1993) *Changing Classroom Cultures: Anti-Racism, Politics and Schools*, Stoke on Trent: Trentham Books.

FERGUSSON, R. (1996) 'Managerialism in education', in CLARKE, J., COCHRANE, A., and McLAUGHLIN, E. (eds) *Managing Social Policy*, London: Sage Publications, pp. 93–114.

FEU (1991) *Quality Matters: Business and Industry Quality Models and Further Education*, London: FEU, August.

FIELDING, M. (1997) 'Beyond school effectiveness and school improvement: lighting the slow fuse of possibility', *The Curriculum Journal*, **8**, 1, 7–27.

FITZ, J., HALPIN, D., and POWER, S. (1993) *Grant Maintained Schools: education in the market place*, London: Kogan Page.

FLEW, A. (1994) *Shephard's Warning: putting education back on course*, London: ASI (Research) Ltd. The Adam Smith Institute.

FOROJALLA, S.B. (1993) *Educational Planning for Development*, London: Macmillan.

FRANZWAY, S., COURT, D., CONNELL, R. (1989) *Staking a Claim: Feminism, Bureaucracy and the State*, Cambridge: Polity Press.

FULLAN, M. (1993) *Changing Forces: Probing the Depth of Educational Reform*, London: Falmer Press.

FULLER, B. (1986) 'Raising school quality in developing countries: what investments boost learning?' *World Bank Discussion Paper No. 2.* Washington DC: World Bank.

FULLER, B. (1987) 'What school factors raise achievement in the Third World?' *Review of Educational Research*, **57**, 3, 255–92.

FULLER, B., and CLARKE, P. (1994) 'Raising school effects while ignoring culture? Local conditions and the influence of classroom tools, rules, and pedagogy, *Review of Educational Research*, **64**, 1, 119–57.

GALTON, M., SIMON, B., and CROLL, P. (1980) *Inside the Primary Classroom*, London: Routledge and Kegan Paul.

GARRAHAN, P., and STEWART, P. (1992) *The Nissan Enigma: Flexibility at Work in a Local Economy*, London: Mansell.

GEWIRTZ, S. (1997) 'Can *all* schools be successful? An exploration of the determinants of school "success"', Paper presented at the British Educational Research Association Annual Conference, York, 11–14 September.

GEWIRTZ, S., BALL, S.J., BOWE, R. (1995) *Markets, Choice and Equity in Education*, Buckingham: Open University Press.

GIBSON, A., and ASTHANA, S. (1998) 'School performance, school effectiveness and the 1997 White Paper', *Oxford Review of Education*, **24**, 2, 195–210.

GIDDENS, A. (1979) *Central Problems in Sociological Theory*, Cambridge: Polity Press.

GIDDENS, A. (1991) *Modernity and Self-Identity: Self and Society in the Late Modern Age*, Cambridge: Polity Press.

GILLBORN, D., and GIPPS, C. (1996) *Recent Research on the Achievements of Ethnic Minority Pupils*, London: Institute of Education/OFSTED.

GILLBORN, D. (1990) *'Race', Ethnicity and Education.* London: Unwin Hyman.

GILLBORN, D. (1997) 'Natural selection? new Labour, race and education policy', *Multicultural Teaching*, **15**, 3, 5–8.

GIROUX, H. (1992) *Border Crossings: Cultural Workers and the Politics of Education*, London: Routledge.

GOLDTHORPE, J. (1996) 'Class analysis and the reorientation of class theory: the case of persisting differentials in educational attainment', *British Journal of Sociology*, **47**, 3, 481–505.

GOODSON, I. (1997) ' "Trendy theory" and teacher professionalism'. *Cambridge Journal of Education*, **27**, 1, 7–22.

GRACE, G. (1995) *School Leadership: Beyond Educational Management*, London: The Falmer Press.

GREENWOOD, M., and GAUNT, H. (1994) *Total Quality Management for Schools*, London: Cassell.

GRIFFITHS, M., and TROYNA, B. (eds), (1995) *Anti-racism, Culture and Social Justice in Education*, Stoke on Trent: Trentham Books.

GRIFFITHS, M. (1998) 'The discourses of social justice in schools', *British Educational Research Journal*, **24**, 3, 301–15.

HADOW, W.H. (1926) *Report of the Consultative Committee of the Board of Education on The Education of the Adolescent*, London: HMSO.

HALL, A. (1974) *The Point of Entry: A Study of Client Reception in the Social Services*, London: Allen and Unwin.

HALL, S. (1983) 'The Great Moving Right Show', in HALL, S., and JACQUES, M. (eds) *The Politics of Thatcherism*, London: Lawrence and Wishart in association with Marxism Today, pp. 19–39.

HALSEY, A., HEATH, A., and RIDGE, J. (1980) *Origins and Destinations: Family, Class and Education in Modern Britain*, Oxford: Clarendon Press.

HAMILTON, D. (1998) 'The idols of the market place', in SLEE, R., WEINER, G., and TOMLINSON, S. (eds), *School Effectiveness for Whom? Challenges to the School Effectiveness and School Improvement Movements*, London: Falmer Press, pp. 13–20.

HARBER, C. (1989) *Politics in African Education*, London: Macmillan.

HARBER, C., and DAVIES, L. (1997) *School Management and Effectiveness in Developing Countries: The Post-Bureaucratic School*, London: Cassell.

HARGREAVES, A., and EVANS, R. (1997) *Beyond Educational Reform*, Buckingham: Open University Press.

HARGREAVES, D. (1967) *Social Relations in a Secondary School*, London: Routledge and Kegan Paul.

HARGREAVES, D. (1984) *Improving Secondary Schools*, Report of the Committee on the Curriculum and Organisation of Secondary Schools, London: Inner London Education Authority.

HARVEY, D. (1989) *The Condition of Postmodernity*, Oxford: Basil Blackwell.

HATCHER, R. (1998a) 'Class differentiation in education: rational choices?' *British Journal of Sociology of Education*, **19**, 1, 5–24.

HATCHER, R. (1998b) 'Social justice and the politics of school effectiveness and improvement', *Race, Ethnicity and Education*, **1**, 2, 267–89.

HATCHER, R., TROYNA, B., and GEWIRTZ, D. (1996) *Racial Equality and the Local Management of Schools*, Stoke-on-Trent: Trentham Books.

HAYEK, F. (1978) *The Mirage of Social Justice*, London: Routledge and Kegan Paul.

HER MAJESTY'S INSPECTORATE, (1978) *Primary Education in England: A Survey by HM Inspectors of Schools*, London: HMSO.

HEYNEMAN, S., and LOXLEY, W. (1983) 'The effects of primary school quality on academic achievement across 29 high and low income countries', *American Journal of Sociology*, **88**, 1162–94.

HEYNEMAN, S. (1986) *The Search for School Effects in Developing Countries: 1966–1986*, Seminar Paper No.33. Washington, DC: International Bank for Reconstruction and Development.

HICKMAN, J., and KIMBERLEY, K. (1988) *Teachers, Language and Learning*, London: Routledge.

HILLGATE GROUP (1986) *Whose Schools? A Radical Manifesto*, London: The Hillgate Group.

HOGGETT, P. (1996) 'New modes of control in the public service'. *Public Administration*, **74**, 9–32.

HOLLAND, J., HAMMER, M., and SHELDON, S. (eds) *Equality and Inequality in Educational Policy*, Clevedon: Multilingual Matters, pp. 281–99.

HOPKINS, D., AINSCOW, M., and WEST, M. (1994) *School Improvement in an Era of Change*, London: Cassell.

HOPKINS, D., AINSCOW, M., and WEST, M. (1996) *Improving the Quality of Education for All*, London: David Fulton Publishers.

HOPPERS, W. (1994) 'Learning the lessons: a thematic review of project experiences', in LITTLE, A., HOPPERS, W., GARDNER, R. (eds), *Beyond Jomtien: Implementing Primary Education for All*, London: Macmillan, pp. 163–86.

HOPPERS, W., and LITTLE, A. (1994) 'Towards a research agenda for primary education in developing countries', in LITTLE, A., HOPPERS, W., GARDNER, R. (eds), *Beyond Jomtien: Implementing Primary Education for All*, London: Macmillan, pp. 211–29.

IMAI, M. (1986) *Kaizen (Ky'zen): The Key to Japan's Competitiveness*, New York: Random House.

JACOBS, J. (1992) *Systems of Survival: A Dialogue on the Moral Functions of Commerce and Politics*, London: Hodder and Stoughton.

JEFFREY, B., and WOODS, P. (1996) 'Feeling deprofessionalized: the social construction of emotions during an OFSTED inspection', *Cambridge Journal of Education*, **26**, 3, 325–43.

JENCKS, C. et al. (1972) *Inequality*, New York: Basic Books.

JONES, K. (1987) *Right Turn: The Conservative Revolution in Education*, London: Hutchinson Radius.

JORA SOL (1985) 'Teaching under apartheid', *Contemporary Issues in Geography and Education*, London: ILEA, 26–27.

JOSEPH, K. (1984) 'North of England conference on education speech, reported "A view from the Top"', in *The Times Educational Supplement*, 13 January 1984.

KENWAY, J., BIGUM, C., and FITZCLARENCE, L. (1993) 'Marketing education in the postmodern age', *Journal of Education Policy*, **8**, 105–22.

KOGAN, M. (1985) 'Education policy and values', in MCNAY, I., and OZGA, J. (eds) *Policy Making in Education*, Oxford: Pergamon Press, pp. 11–23.

KOTEEN, J. (1997) *Strategic Management in Public and Non-Profit Organizations: Managing Public Concerns in an Era of Limits*, West Port, Connecticut and London: Praeger.

KOWSZUN, J. (1992) *Soft-systems methodology: an approach to problem-solving in the management of education*, Mendip Papers, Bristol: The Staff College.

LACEY, C. (1970) *Hightown Grammar*, Manchester: Manchester University Press.

LANG, P., and MARLAND, M. (eds), (1985) *New directions in pastoral care*, Oxford: Blackwell in association with the National Association for Pastoral Care in Education and the Economic and Social Research Council.

LAUDER, H., JAMIESON, I., WIKELEY, F. (1998) 'Models of effective schools: limits and capabilities', in SLEE, R., WEINER, G., and TOMLINSON, S. (eds), *School Effectiveness for Whom? Challenges to the School Effectiveness and School Improvement Movements*, London: The Falmer Press, pp. 51–69.

LE GRAND, J. (1991) *Equity and Choice: An Essay in Economics and Applied Philosophy*, London: HarperCollins.

LEVACIC, R. (1993) 'The co-ordination of the school system', in MAIDMENT, R., and THOMPSON, G. (eds), *Managing the UK*, London: Sage.

LEVIN, H., and LOCKHEED, M. (eds), (1993) *Effective Schools in Developing Countries*, London: Falmer Press.

LIPIETZ, A. (1979) *Towards a New Economic Order: Post-Fordism, Ecology and Democracy*, Cambridge: Polity Press.

LIPIETZ, A. (1994) 'Post-Fordism and democracy', in AMIN, A. (ed.) *Post-Fordism: A Reader*, Oxford: Basil Blackwell, pp. 338–58.

LOCKHEED, M., and VERSPOOR, A. (1991) *Improving Primary Education in Developing Countries*, Oxford: World Bank/Oxford University Press.

LOCKHEED, M. (1993) 'The condition of primary education in developing countries', in LEVIN, H., and LOCKHEED, M. (eds) *Effective Schools in Developing Countries*, London: Falmer, pp. 20–40.

MACLURE, S.J. (1982) *Educational Documents: England and Wales 1816 to the present day*, [for documentation of The Newcastle Commission (1861) and The Revised Code (1862)], London: Methuen.

MAIDMENT, R., and THOMPSON, G. (eds) (1993) *Managing the United Kingdom*, London: Sage.

MARLAND, M. (1974) *Pastoral care: organizing the care and guidance of the individual pupil in a comprehensive school*, London: Heinemann.

MARSDEN, D. (1971) *Politicians, Equality and Comprehensives*, T. 411, London: Fabian Society.

MARSLAND, D. (1995) *Self-Reliance*, London: Transaction Publishers.

MASSEY, D., and ALLEN, J. (1992) *The Economy in Question: Restructuring Britain*, London: Sage.

McGREW, A. (1992) 'A global society?' in HALL, S., HELD, D., and McGREW, T. (eds) *Modernity and Its Futures*, Cambridge: Polity Press.

McNAIR, C.J., and LEIBFRIED, K.H.J. (1992) *Benchmarking: A Tool for Continuous Improvement*, Essex Junction: Oliver Wight Publications.

MINISTRY of EDUCATION (1963) *Half Our Future (The Newsom Report)*, London: HMSO.

MOI, T. (1991) 'Appropriating Bourdieu: feminist theory and Pierre Bourdieu's sociology of culture', *New Literary History*, **22**, 1017–49.

MORLEY, L. (1995) 'Empowerment and the New Right', *Youth and Policy*, **51**(Winter), 1–10.

MORLEY, L. (1997a) 'Change and equity in Higher Education', *British Journal of Sociology of Education*, **18**, 2, 231–42.

Morley, L. (1997b) 'A class of one's own: women, social class and the academy', in Mahony, P., and Zmroczek, C. (eds), *Class Matters*, London: Taylor and Francis.

Morley, L. (1998a) 'All you need is love: feminist pedagogy for empowerment and emotional labour in the academy', *International Journal of Inclusive Education*, **2**, 1, 15–27.

Morley, L. (1998b) 'Equity, empowerment and school effectiveness', in Prakesh, V. (ed.), *Teacher Empowerment and School Effectiveness at Primary Stage*, New Delhi, India: National Council of Educational Research and Training, pp. 403–16.

Morley, L. (1999) *Organising Feminisms: The Micropolitics of the Academy*, London: Macmillan.

Mortimore, P. et al. (1988) *School Matters: The Junior Years*, Wells: Open Books.

Mortimore, P., and Whitty, G. (1997) *Can School Improvement Overcome the Effects of Disadvantage?* London: Institute of Education.

Murgatroyd, S., and Morgan, C. (1992) *Total Quality Management and the School*, Buckingham: Open University Press.

National Union of Teachers (1992) *NUT Survey on Pupils' Exclusions: information from LEAs*, London: NUT.

Nehaul, K. (1996) *The Schooling of Children of Caribbean Heritage*, Stoke-on-Trent: Trentham Books.

Ngugi wa Thiongo (1993) 'The language of African literature', in Williams, P., and Chrisman, L. (eds) *Colonial Discourse and Post-Colonial Theory: A Reader*, London: Harvester Wheatsheaf, pp. 435–55.

O'Brien, M., and Whitmore, E. (1989) 'Empowering women students in Higher Education', *McGill Journal of Education*, **24**, 3, 305–20.

OECD (1989a) *Education and the Economy in a Changing Society*, Paris: OECD.

OECD (1989b) *Schools and Quality: An International Report*, Paris: OECD.

OECD (1994) *School: A Matter of Choice*, Paris: OECD.

Office for Standards in Education (OFSTED) (1993) *Education for Disaffected Pupils*, London: HMSO.

Office for Standards in Education (OFSTED) (1996a) *The Gender Divide: Performance Differences Between Boys and Girls at School*, London: HMSO.

Office for Standards in Education (OFSTED) (1996b) *Exclusions from Secondary Schools*, London: HMSO.

Okun, A. (1975) *Equality and Efficiency: The Big Trade*, Washington, DC: Brookings.

Olowe, S. (ed.) (1990) *Against the Tide: Black Experience in the ILEA*, London: Hansin Books.

Owens, R.G. (1991) *Organizational Behavior in Education*, Needham Heights, MA: Allyn and Bacon.

Oxenham, J. with DeJong, J., and Treagust, S. (1990) 'Improving the quality of education in developing countries', in Griffin, K., and Knight, J. (eds) *Human Development and the International Development Strategy for the 1990s*, London: Macmillan, pp. 101–27.

Parker, S. (1997) *Reflective Teaching in the Postmodern World*, Buckingham: Open University Press.

Parry, G. et al. (1987) 'The crowd and the community: context, content and aftermath', in Gaskell, G., and Benewick, R. (eds) *The Crowd in Contemporary Britain*, London: Sage.

PECHEUX, M. (1982) *Language, Semantics and Ideology: Stating the Obvious*, London: Macmillan.

PENNYCUICK, D. (1993) *School Effectiveness in Developing Countries: A Summary of the Research Evidence*, London: Overseas Development Agency.

PETERS, T., and WATERMAN, R. (1995) *In Search of Excellence: Lessons From America's Best-Run Companies*, London: Harper Collins Publishers.

PIORE, M., and SABEL, C. (1984) *The Second Industrial Divide: Possibilities for Prosperity*, New York: Basic Books.

PLOWDEN, B. (1967) *Children and Their Primary Schools: Report of the Central Advisory Council for Education (England)*, London: HMSO.

POLLERT, A. (1988) 'Dismantling flexibility', *Capital and Class*, **34**, Spring, 42–75.

POLLITT, C. (1993) *Managerialism and the Public Services: Cuts or Cultural Change in the 1990s* (2nd edn), Oxford: Blackwell.

POWER, M. (1994) *The Audit Explosion*, London: Demos.

RAMASUT, A., and REYNOLDS, D. (1993) 'Developing effective whole school approaches to special educational needs: From school effectiveness theory to school development practice', In SLEE, R. (ed.), *Is There a Desk with My Name on It?*, London: Falmer Press.

RANSON, S., and STEWART, J. (1994) *Management for the Public Domain: Enabling the Learning Society*, London: Macmillan.

RASSOOL, N. (1993) 'Post-Fordism? Technology and new forms of control: the case of technology in the curriculum', *British Journal of Sociology of Education*, **14**, 3, 227–44.

RASSOOL, N. (1995) 'Language, cultural pluralism and the silencing of minority discourses in England and Wales', *Journal of Educational Policy*, **10**, 3, 287–302.

RASSOOL, N. (1999) *Literacy for Sustainable Development in the Age of Information*, Clevedon, Avon: Multilingual Matters.

REA, J., and WEINER, G. (1998) 'Cultures of blame and redemption – when empowerment becomes control: practitioners' views of the effective schools movement', in SLEE, R., WEINER, G., and TOMLINSON, S. (eds), *School Effectiveness for Whom? Challenges to the School Effectiveness and School Improvement Movements*, London: The Falmer Press, pp. 21–32.

REAY, D. (1996) 'Contextualising choice: social power and parental involvement', *British Educational Research Journal*, **22**, 5, 581–96.

REAY, D. (1998) 'Micro-politics in the 1990s: Staff relationships in secondary schooling', *Journal of Education Policy*, **13**, 2, 179–96.

REAY, D., and BALL, S.J. (1997) 'Spoilt for choice': The working classes and educational markets', *Oxford Review of Education*, **23**, 1, 89–101.

REYNOLDS, D. (1991) 'School effectiveness in secondary schools: research and its policy implications', in RIDDELL, S., and BROWN, S. (eds) *School Effectiveness Research: Its Messages for School Improvement*, Edinburgh: The Scottish Office, pp. 21–33.

REYNOLDS, D., and SULLIVAN, M. (1987) *The Comprehensive Experience*, Lewes: The Falmer Press.

REYNOLDS, D., et al. (eds) (1996) *Making Good Schools: Linking School Effectiveness and School Improvement*, London: Routledge.

RHEINGOLD, H. (1993) *The Virtual Community*, Reading, MA: Addison-Wesley.

RICHARDSON, D. (1998) 'Sexuality and citizenship', *Sociology*, **32**, 1, 83–100.

RIDDELL, S., and BROWN, S. (ed.), (1991) *School Effectiveness Research: Its Messages for School Improvement*, Edinburgh: The Scottish Office.

ROBBINS, LORD, (1963) *Report of the Committee on Higher Education*, London: HMSO.

ROBINSON, H.A. (1994) *The Ethnography of Empowerment: The Transformative Power of Classroom Interaction*, London and Washington: Taylor and Francis.

RONDINELLI, D.A. (1993) *Development Projects as Policy Experiments: an adaptive approach to development administration*, London and New York: Routledge.

ROSE, M. (1995) *Possible Lives – The Promise of Public Education in America*, New York: Penguin Books.

ROSENHOLTZ, S. (1989) *Teachers' Workplace: The Social Organisation of Schools*, New York: Longman.

ROSTOW, W.W. (1966) *The Stages of Economic Growth: a Non-Communist Manifesto*, London: Cambridge University Press.

ROWNTREE FOUNDATION (1995) *Inquiry into Income and Wealth*, chaired by Sir Peter Bailey, York: Joseph Rowntree Foundation.

RUBAGUMYA, C.M. (ed.) (1990) *Language in Education in Africa: A Tanzanian Perspective*, Clevedon: Multilingual Matters.

RUTTER, M. et al. (1979) *Fifteen Thousand Hours*, Cambridge, MA: Harvard University Press.

RYAN, J. (1995) 'The new institutionalism in postmodern times: de-differentiation and the study of institutions', *Politics of Education Yearbook*, pp. 189–202.

SABEL, C.F. (1984) *Work and Politics: The Division of Labor in Industry*, Cambridge: Cambridge University Press.

SAID, E. (1984) *The World, The Text and The Critic*, London: Faber.

SALLIS, E. (1993) *Total Quality Management in Education*, London: Kogan Page.

SAMMONS, P., HILLMAN, J., MORTIMORE, P. (1995) *Key Characteristics of Effective Schools: A Review of School Effectiveness Research*, London: Institute of Education/Office for Standards in Education.

SAMMONS, P., THOMAS, S., MORTIMORE, P. (1995) 'Accounting for variations in academic effectiveness between schools and departments', in *ECER/ BERA Annual Conference*, Bath: Institute of Education, University of London.

SCHON, D. (1983) *The Reflective Practitioner*, London: Temple Smith.

SCHULTZ, T.W. (1963) *The Economic Value of Education*, New York: Columbia Press.

SCHULTZ, T. (1979) *The Economic Value of Education*, New York: Columbia University Press.

SENGE, P. (1990) *The Fifth Discipline: The Art and Practice of the Learning Organization*, New York: Doubleday.

SENGE, P.M., KLEINER, A., ROBERTS, C., ROSS, R., and SMITH, B. (1994) *The Fifth Discipline Fieldbook: Strategies and Tools for Building a Learning Organization*, New York: Doubleday.

SHAVIT, Y., and BLOSSFELD, H.P. (eds) (1993) *Persistent Inequality: Changing Educational Attainment in Thirteen Countries*, Boulder: Westview Press.

SHAW, J. (1995) *Education, Gender and Anxiety*, London: Taylor and Francis.

SHAW, K. (1990) 'Ideology, control and the teaching profession', *Policy and Politics*, **18**, 4, 269–78.

SHREWSBURY, C. (1987) 'What is feminist pedagogy?' *Women's Studies Quarterly*, **XV**, 3 and 4, 6–14.

References

SKEGGS, B. (1997) *Formations of Class and Gender*, London: Sage.

SKELTON, C. (1998) 'Feminism and research into masculinities and schooling', *Gender and Education*, **10**, 2, 217–27.

SKILBECK, M. (ed.), (1984) *Readings in School-based Curriculum Development*, London: Harper Education.

SLAVIN, R.E. (1996) *Education for All*, Lisse: Swets and Zeitlinger.

SLEE, R. (1998) 'High reliability organizations and liability students – the politics of recognition', in SLEE, R., WEINER, G., and TOMLINSON, S. (eds) *School Effectiveness for Whom? Challenges to the School Effectiveness and School Improvement Movements*, London: The Falmer Press, pp. 101–14.

SLEE, R., and WEINER, G. (1998) 'Introduction: school effectiveness for whom?' in SLEE, R., WEINER, G., and TOMLINSON, S. (eds) *School Effectiveness for Whom? Challenges to the School Effectiveness and School Improvement Movements*, London: The Falmer Press, pp. 1–9.

SMITH, T., and NOBLE, M. (1995) *Education Divides: Poverty and Schooling in the 1990s*, London: CPAG.

SOUTHWORTH, G. (1994) 'The learning school', RIBBINS, P., and BURRIDGE, E. (eds) *Improving Education: promoting quality in schools*, London: Cassell, pp. 52–73.

SOUTHWORTH, G. (1996) 'Improving primary schools: shifting the emphasis and clarifying the focus', *School Organisation*, **16**, 3, 263–80.

SPENDER, D. (1982) *Invisible Women: The Schooling Scandal*, London: Writers and Readers Co-operative.

SPENS, W. (1938) *Report of the Consultative Committee of the Board of Education on Secondary Education with Special Reference to Grammar Schools and Technical High Schools*, London: HMSO.

STENHOUSE, L. (1975) *An Introduction to Curriculum Research and Development*, London: Heinemann.

STEWART, F. (1994) 'Education and adjustment: the experience of the 1980s and lessons for the 1990s', in PRENDERGAST, R., and STEWART, F. (eds) *Market Forces and World Development*, Basingstoke: The Macmillan Press, pp. 128–59.

STOLL, L., and FINK, D. (1996) *Changing Our Schools: Linking School Effectiveness with School Improvement*, Buckingham: Open University Press.

STRATHERN, M. (1997) ' "Improving ratings": audit in the British university system', *European Review*, **5**, 3, 305–21.

SWANN COMMITTEE, (1985) *Education for All: the report of a committee of inquiry into the education of children from ethnic minority groups*, Cmnd 9453, Department of Education and Science, London: HMSO.

TAYLOR, C. (1977) *A New Partnership for Our Schools*. London: Department of Education and Science.

THOMSON, R. (1995) 'Unholy alliances: the recent politics of sex education', in DAWTREY, L., HAMMER, M., and SHELDON, S. (ed.), *Equality and Inequality in Education Policy*, Clevedon: Multilingual Matters, pp. 281–99.

THRUPP, M. (1998) 'The art of the possible: organizing and managing high and low socio economic schools', *Journal of Education Policy*, **13**, 2, 197–219.

TIZZARD, B. et al. (1988) *Young Children at School in the Inner City*, Hove: Lawrence Erlbaum Associates.

TOMANEY, J. (1990) 'The reality of work place flexibility', *Capital and Class*, **40**, Spring, 29–60.

TOMANEY, J. (1994) 'A new paradigm of work organization and technology?' in AMIN, A. *Post-Fordism: A Reader*, Oxford: Basil Blackwell, pp. 157–94.

TOMLINSON, S. (1987) 'Curriculum option choices in multi-ethnic schools', TROYNA, B. (ed.), *Racial Inequality in Education*, London: Tavistock, pp. 92–108.

TOMLINSON, S. (1998) 'A tale of one school in one city: Hackney Downs', in SLEE, R., WEINER, G., and TOMLINSON, S. (eds) *School Effectiveness for Whom?* London: The Falmer Press, pp. 157–69.

TRAVERS, C.J., and COOPER, C.L. (1996) *Teachers Under Pressure: Stress in the Teaching Profession*, London: Routledge.

TROYNA, B., and SIRAJ-BLATCHFORD, I. (1993) 'Providing support or denying access? The experiences of students designated as "ESL" and "SN" in a multi-ethnic secondary school', *Educational Review*, **45**, 1, 3–11.

VAIZEY, J., and DEBEAUVAIS, M. (1961) 'Economic aspects of educational development', in HALSEY, A.H., FLOUD, J., and ANDERSON, C.A. (eds) *Education, Economy and Society: A Reader in the Sociology of Education*, London: Macmillan Press.

VAIZEY, J. (1958) *The Costs of Education*, London: Allen and Unwin.

VAIZEY, J. (1962) *The Control of Education*, London: Faber and Faber.

VAIZEY, J. (1967) *Education for Tomorrow*, London: Penguin Books.

WALKER, R., and ADELMAN, C. (1975) *A Guide to Classroom Observation*, London: Methuen and Co.

WALKERDINE, V. (1995) 'Subject to change without notice: psychology, postmodernity and the popular', in PILE, S., and THRIFT, N. (eds) *Mapping the Subject: Geographies of Cultural Transformation*, London: Routledge, pp. 309–31.

WALKERDINE, V. (1997) 'Keynote address at the Gender and Education International Conference', University of Warwick, April, 1997.

WARNOCK, M. (1978) *Report on the Enquiry into the Education of Handicapped Children and Young People*, London: Department of Education and Science.

WATKINS, P. (1994) 'The Fordist/Post-Fordist debate: the educational implications', in KENWAY, J. (ed.) *Economising Education: The Post-Fordist Directions*, Geelong: Deakin University Press.

WEEKS, J. (1991) 'Pretended family relationships', in CLARKE, D. (ed.) *Marriage, Domestic Life and Social Change*, London: Routledge.

WEILER, K. (1988) *Women Teaching for Change*, South Hadley, MA: Bergin and Garvey.

WEINER, G. (1994) *Feminisms in Education*, Buckingham: Open University Press.

WHITTY, G. POWER, S., and EDWARDS, T. (1998) 'The assisted places scheme: its impact and its role in privatization and marketization', *Journal of Education Policy*, **13**, 2, 237–50.

WHITTY, G., POWER, S., and HALPIN, D. (1997) *Devolution and Choice in Education*, Buckingham: Open University.

WILCOX, B. (1997) 'Schooling, school improvement and the relevance of Alasdair MacIntyre', *Cambridge Journal of Education*, **27**, 2, 249–60.

WILLIAMS, R. (1961) *The Long Revolution*, Harmondsworth: Penguin Books in association with Chatto and Windus.

WILLIAMS, R. (1976) *Keywords: A Vocabulary of Culture and Society*, Glasgow: Fontana.

WILLIAMS, R. (1989) 'Hegemony and the Selective Tradition'. In CASTELL, S. de LUKE, A., and LUKE, C. (eds) *Language, Authority and Criticism: Readings on the School Textbook*, Lewes: Falmer Press, pp. 56–60.

References

WILLIS, P. (1977) *Learning to Labour: How Working Class Kids Get Working Class Jobs*, Farnborough: Saxon House.

WINCH, C. (1996) 'Equality, quality and diversity', *Journal of Philosophy of Education*, **30**, 1, 113–28.

WOLF, W. (1984) 'Invasion of robots threatens labor, *International Viewpoint*, **45**, 30, 22–3.

WOODS, P. (1992) 'Empowerment through choice? Towards an understanding of parental choice and school responsiveness', *Education Management and Administration*, **20**, 4, 204–11.

WOODS, P., JEFFREY, B., TROMAN, G., and BOYLE, M. (1997) *Restructuring Schools, Restructuring Teachers*, Buckingham: Open University Press.

WORLD BANK (1988) *Education in Sub-Saharan Africa: Policies for Adjustment, Revitalization and Expansion*, Washington: The World Bank.

WORLD BANK (1990) *Primary Education: A World Bank Policy Paper*, Washington: The World Bank.

WORLD BANK (1995) *Priorities and Strategies for Education: A World Bank Review*, Washington: The World Bank.

WRIGHT, C. (1986) 'School processes – an ethnographic study', in EGGLESTON, J., DUNN, D., and ANJALI, M. (eds) *Education for Some: The Educational and Vocational Experiences of 15–18 year old Members of Minority Ethnic Groups*, Stoke-on-Trent: Trentham Books.

YOSHIMURA, N., and ANDERSON, P. (1997) *Inside the Kaisha: Demystifying Japanese Business Behavior*, Boston, Mass.: Harvard Business School Press.

Index